... I have to beg. I'd be closer, closer to you. Closer, got to get closer, closer to you

... that I must tell. It's started just being round your leg. When I was dreaming

... is nothing. Changing decorate your lips. Closer, closer, closer to you. Closer, get

... what. Pushed down your front. When you feel the time was right, I'd

... you. Closer, closer, closer to, round your bed. Right next to your skin. ...

... Closer, closer, closer to you. If I had my wishes. If I had my way I

... you walking by. Closer. Wish I was a ... Changing to after the

... I have to beg. I'd be closer, closer to you. Closer, got to get closer, closer to you

I was a necklace Hanging decorate your lips Closer closer closer to you Closer ...

...was a naked line Dripped down your front When you feel the heat was right I ...

...you Closer closer closer to round your bed Right next to your heart Tops ...

...ing Closer closer closer to you If I had my wishes If I had my way I'd be all ...

...ing a walking by Closer Rich I was a stocking Clinging to your legs Eve...

...wouldn't have to beg I'd be there always to you Closer get to get closer closer to yo...

...tightened lines If I was a skirt I'd ... just being around your leg When I ...

Henry V

莎翁戏剧经典

亨利五世

〔英〕威廉·莎士比亚 著
支荩忠 注释

商务印书馆
The Commercial Press
SINCE 1897
2016年·北京

威廉·莎士比亚

图 1

图 2（见 6 页）

PROLOGUE

Enter CHORUS.

CHORUS.

O for a Muse of fire, that would ascend
The brightest heaven of invention, —
A kingdom for a stage, princes to act,
And monarchs to behold the swelling scene!

图 3（见 10 页）

London. An ante-chamber in the KING'S *palace.*

Enter the ARCHBISHOP OF CANTERBURY *and the* BISHOP OF ELY.

ARCHBISHOP OF CANTERBURY.

My lord, I'll tell you, —that self bill is urged,
Which in th' eleventh year of the last king's reign
Was like, and had indeed against us past,
But that the scambling and unquiet time
Did push it out of further question.

图 4（见 18 页）

The same. The Presence-chamber.

Enter KING HENRY, GLOSTER, BEDFORD, EXETER, WARWICK, WESTMORELAND, *and* ATTENDANTS.

KING HENRY.

Where is my gracious Lord of Canterbury?

DUKE OF EXETER.

Not here in presence.

KING HENRY.

Send for him, good uncle.

图 5（见 34 页）

KING HENRY.
We are no tyrant, but a Christian king;
Unto whose grace our passion is as subject
As are our wretches fetter'd in our prisons.

图 6（见 38 页）

KING HENRY.

Therefore let every man now task his thought,
That this fair action may on foot be brought.

图 7（见 40 页）

CHORUS.

Now all the youth of England are on fire,
And silken dalliance in the wardrobe lies：
Now thrive the armorers，and honor's thought
Reigns solely in the breast of every man：
...

图 8（见 42 页）

London. Befor the Boar's Head Tavern, Eastcheap.
Enter CORPORAL NYM *and* LIEUTENANT BARDOLPH.

BARDOLPH.
Well met, Corporal Nym.

NYM.
Good morrow, Lieutenant Bardolph.

图 9（见 48 页）

BOY.

Mine host Pistol, you must come to my master, ...

图 10（见 82 页）

FRENCH KING.

You shall be soon dispatcht with fair conditions.
A night is but small breath and little pause
To answer matters of this consequence.

图 11（见 84 页）

CHORUS.

Suppose that you have seen
The well-appointed king at Hampton pier
Embark his royalty; and his brave fleet
With silken streamers the young Phœbus fanning:

图 **12**（见 86 页）

Alarums. Enter KING HENRY, EXETER, BEDFORD, GLOSTER, *and* SOLDIERS, *with scaling-ladders.*

KING HENRY.

Once more unto the breach, dear friends, once more;
Or close the wall up with our English dead! …
Follow your spirit: and, upon this charge,
Cry 'God for Harry, England, and Saint George!'

图 13（见 88 页）

France. Before Harfleur

Enter NYM, BARDOLPH, PISTOL, *and* BOY.

BARDOLPH.

On, on, on, on, on! to the breach, to the breach!

图 14（见 102 页）

The French KING's *palace*.

Enter KATHARINE *and* ALICE.

KATHARINE.

Alice, tu as été en Angleterre, et tu parles bien le langage.

ALICE.

Un peu, madame.

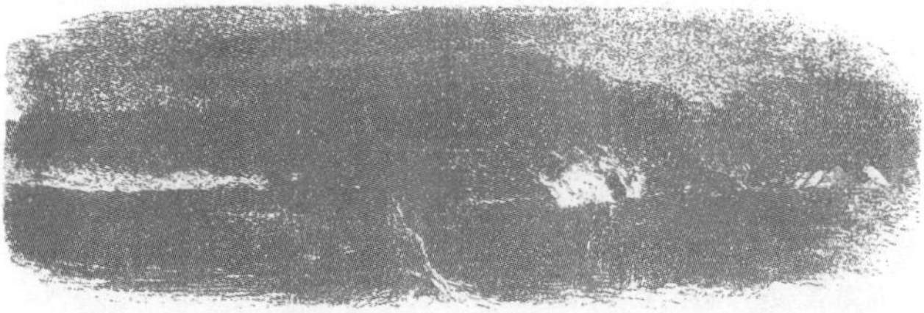

图 **15**（见 138 页）

DUKE OF ORLEANS.

It is now two o'clock: but, let me see, — by ten
We shall have each a hundred Englishmen.

图 16（见 140 页）

CHORUS.

Now entertain conjecture of a tiem
When creeping murmur and the poring dark
Fills the wide vessel of the universe.
From camp to camp, through the foul womb of night,
The hum of either army stilly sounds,
That the fixt sentinels almost receive
The secret whispers of each other's watch:
...

图 17（见 144 页）

The English camp at Agincourt.

Enter KING HENRY, BEDFORD, *and* GLOSTER.

KING HENRY.

Gloster, 'tis true that we are in great danger;
The greater therefore should our courage be.—

图 18（见 166 页）

KING HENRY.

Not to-day, O Lord,
O, not to-day, think not upon the fault
My father made in compassing the crown!
I Richard's body have interred new;
And on it have bestow'd more contrite tears
Than from it issued forced drops of blood:
…

图 19（见 166 页）

The French camp.

Enter the DAUPHIN, ORLEANS, RAMBURES, *and others.*

DUKE OF ORLEANS.

The sun doth gild our armor; up, my lords!

DAUPHIN.

Montez à cheval! — My horse! *varlet*, *laquais*! ha!

图 20（见 182 页）

The field of battle.

Alarum: excursions. Enter PISTOL, *French* SOLDIER, *and* BOY.

PISTOL.

Yield, cur!

FRENCH SOLDIER.

Je pense que vous êtes le gentilhomme de bonne qualité.

图 21（见 218 页）

KING HENRY.

Do we all holy rites：
Let there be sung *Non nobis* and *Te Deum*.
The dead with charity enclosed in clay，…

图 22（见 220 页）

CHORUS.

…Now we bear the king
Towards Calais: grant him there; there seen,
Heave him away upon your winged thoughts
Athwart the sea. Behold, the English beach
Pales in the flood with men, with wives, and boys,
Whose shouts and claps out-voice the deep-mouth'd sea,
…

图 **23**（见 222 页）

France. The English camp.

Enter FLUELLEN *and* GOWER.

GOWER.

Nay, that's right; but why wear you your leek to-day? Saint Davy's day is past.

图 24（见 230 页）

France. The French KING'S *palace.*

Enter, at one door, KING HENRY, BEDFORD, GLOSTER, EXETER, WARWICK, WESTMORELAND, *and other* LORDS; *at another, the French* KING, QUEEN ISABEL, *the* PRINCESS KATHARINE, ALICE, *other* LADIES, *and* LORDS; *the* DUKE OF BURGUNDY, *and his* TRAIN.

KING HENRY.

Peace to this meeting, wherefore we are met!
Unto our brother France, and to our sister,
Health and fair time of day; — joy and good wishes
To our most fair and princely cousin Katharine; —

图 25（见 256 页）

CHORUS.

Thus far, with rough and all unable pen.
Our bending author hath pursued the story;

“莎翁戏剧经典”丛书总序

莎士比亚（William Shakespeare，1564—1616）是英国 16 世纪文艺复兴时期的伟大剧作家和诗人，也是世界文坛上的巨擘。他一生创作了 38 部戏剧作品（一说 37 部），诗作包括两部长篇叙事诗、一部十四行诗集以及其他一些短篇诗作。四百多年来这些作品被翻译成多种文字，在世界各地广泛传播。正如他同时代的批评家和剧作家本·琼生所说，他是“时代的灵魂”，“不属于一个时代，而属于所有的时代！”莎士比亚在世期间，他的戏剧作品曾吸引了大量观众，包括宫廷王室成员和普通百姓，产生了巨大影响。18 世纪以来，这些作品始终活跃在舞台上，20 世纪随着电影业的发展，它们又被搬上银幕。几百年来，无论是体现莎士比亚原作的表演还是经过不断改编的作品，莎剧都拥有众多的观者，散发出不灭的艺术光辉；另一方面，自 1623 年莎士比亚全集第一对开本问世，莎士比亚的戏剧也成为学者和广大普通读者阅读、学习、研究的对象，在历代读者的阅读和研究中，这些作品不断得到新阐释和挖掘。莎士比亚的作品焕发着永久不衰的生命活力。

1564 年 4 月，莎士比亚出生于英格兰中部的埃文河畔的斯特拉福镇。家境殷实，父亲曾经营手套和羊毛，并做过小镇的镇长。莎士比亚小时曾在镇上的文法学校读书，受到过较为正规的拉丁文和古典文学的教育。不久，家道中落，陷入经济困境，这可能成为莎士比亚后来未能进入大学读书的原因。1582 年，莎士比亚十八岁时与邻村一位大他八岁的女子安·哈撒韦成婚，六个月后，大女儿苏珊娜降生，此后他们又有了一对孪生子女，不幸的是，儿子哈姆内特早夭。16 世纪 90 年代左右，莎士比亚来到伦敦，发展他的戏剧事业。他曾是剧团的演员、编剧和股东。90 年代初期，莎士比亚即开始戏剧创作。1592 年，莎士比亚已在同行中崭露头角，被当时的“大学才子”剧作家格林所嫉妒，他把莎士比亚称作“那只新抖起来的乌鸦”，“借我们的羽毛来打扮自己……狂妄地幻想着能独自震撼(Shake-scene)这个国家的舞台”。1592—1594 年间，伦敦因流行瘟疫，大部分剧院关闭，在此期间莎士比亚完成了两部著名的长篇叙事诗《维纳斯与阿多尼斯》与《鲁克丽丝受辱记》。1594 年剧院恢复营业之后，莎士比亚加入宫廷大臣剧团，并终生服务于该剧团，直到 1613 年离开伦敦返回家乡。90 年代中期，他进入了戏剧创作的巅峰时期。在 1590 年至 1613 年的二十多年之间，莎士比亚共创作了历史剧、悲剧、喜剧、传奇剧等 38 部。90 年代中后期，他的创作以喜剧和历史剧为主，包括喜剧《仲夏夜之梦》(1595)、《威尼斯商人》(1596)、《无事生非》(1598—1599)、《皆大欢喜》(1599—1600)等和大部分历史剧，如《理查三世》(1592—1593)、《亨利四世》(上、下)(1596—1598)、《亨利五世》(1598—1599)等。这一时期，他的创作风格较为明快，充满积极向上的格调，即便剧中有悲剧的成分，整个作品也透露出对生活的肯定，对理想的向往，如《罗密欧与朱丽叶》(1595)。进入 17 世纪后，莎士比亚的戏剧更多地转向对人生重大问题的思考，探索解决人生之困顿的途径，诸如权力、欲望、嫉妒、暴政等等。四大悲剧《哈姆莱特》(1600—1601)、《奥瑟罗》(1603—1604)、《李尔王》(1605—1606)、《麦克白》(1606)均完成于这一时期。此外，几部重要的罗马题材剧也在 90 年代末和新世纪的最初几年完成，如《裘力斯・凯撒》(1599)、《安东尼与克里奥佩特拉》(1606)、《科里奥兰纳斯》(1608)等。莎士比亚这一时期也创作了几部喜剧，但风格较前一时期更多悲情色彩，更为沉重而引人深思。1609 年，莎士比亚《十四行诗集》出版。晚期的莎士比亚剧作风格有一定变化，最有影响的是传奇剧，如《暴风雨》，通过想象的世界与现实世界的对照来探讨人生问题。

莎士比亚的名字开始传入中国是在 19 世纪中上叶，他的戏剧被翻译成汉语而为国人所知则是在 20 世纪初期。当时，他剧作的内容通过英国 19 世纪兰姆姐弟《莎士比亚戏剧故事集》的汉译被介绍到中国来,即无译者署名的《澥外奇谭》(1903)和林纾、魏易翻译的《吟边燕语》(1904)。20 世纪 20 年代,莎剧汉译事业的开拓者田汉翻译了《哈孟雷特》(1921)和《罗密欧与朱丽叶》(1924)。此后,朱生豪、梁实秋、孙大雨、曹禺、曹未风、虞尔昌等译家都翻译过莎士比亚的剧作。朱生豪先生在经历日本侵略的苦难、贫穷和疾病折磨的极其艰苦的环境下,以惊人的毅力和顽强的意志,克服种种艰难险阻,穷毕生之精力完成了 31 部半莎剧的翻译,成为播撒莎士比亚文明之火的普罗米修斯,译莎事业的英雄和圣徒。他的莎剧译文优美畅达,人物性格鲜明,成为广大读者所珍爱的艺术瑰宝。梁实秋是中国迄今为止唯一一位个人独立完成莎剧和莎诗汉译工程的翻译家。梁译有详尽的注释和说明,学术含量较高。1956 年,卞之琳翻译的《哈姆雷特》出版,他完善了孙大雨提出的翻译原则,提出“以顿代步、韵式依原诗、等行翻译”的翻译方法,可谓开一代诗体译法之风,他的译本至今都被视作该剧最优秀的译本。方平是另一位重要的成绩卓著的莎剧翻译家。2000 年由他主编主译的《新莎士比亚全集》出版,其中 25 部莎剧由方平翻译,其他作品由阮坤、吴兴华、汪义群、覃学岚、屠岸、张冲等译出,为国内目前首部全部由分行诗体翻译的莎剧莎诗全集。

时至今日,莎士比亚的戏剧作品仍不断有新的译本出版,对广大读者而言,阅读汉译的莎剧已经是一件十分方便的事情,而这些汉译莎剧作品中不乏优秀的译本。然而,尽管莎剧的汉译丰富多彩,莎剧的改编层出不穷,要想真正了解莎剧的本来面目,我们还需要回到莎剧原文本身。其中的原因有三:一、每一种语言都是丰富的,其表达的意义可能是多元多面的,但由于译出语和译入语两种语言之间的差异,再好的翻译也只能尽可能地贴近原文而不可能百分之百地再现原文的魅力,因此,阅读再好的译本也无法取代或等同于阅读原作;二、莎士比亚生活的时代距今已经有约 400 年,他所使用的英语与今天人们所熟悉的英语已有较大差异,当时的人们所熟悉的文化和历史事件也是我们今天并不熟知的,因此,要真正领悟他的作品,还需回到他那时的语言和文化中去；三、莎剧经过约400年的变迁，在改编中不断变换，有些已经走出了莎士比亚时代的莎剧，因而，想要认识和了解莎剧，最佳的办法还是回到莎剧的原文本中去。

莎士比亚生活和创作的时期在16世纪末17世纪初。英语在当时已经得到极大的发展，十分活跃而成熟，尤其莎士比亚戏剧中所运用的英语，文辞丰富、结构灵活、表达力很强。但随着时代的发展，其中的一些用词、用语以及语义等都发生了变化，与我们今天的英语存在一定距离，理解起来也就会有一定困难。莎剧在绝大多数情况下采用的是诗体写作，即人物的语言是分行的，每行十个音节，轻重音节相间，一轻一重的每两个音节构成一个音步，不押韵，因此，他的剧作均为抑扬格五音步的素体诗。这样的诗体形式突显出莎剧语言的艺术魅力，音韵优美、铿锵，节奏感强，表达生动有力。然而，正因为这是诗体写作，在语法上就可能出现诗语言特有的结构，比如倒装句或词序颠倒的现象等。莎剧的语言丰富多彩，不同人物的话语呈现出多种特色，时而体现出古典拉丁语的文风，时而出现双关语、俚语、隐喻等修辞手法。典故、历史事件、政治元素、宗教、生活习俗等等都可能成为今天的读者理解莎剧原文本的障碍。因而，借助良好的注释来理解莎剧的原作就成为我们了解和认识莎剧原貌的必要手段。这次由商务印书馆隆重推出的“莎翁戏剧经典”丛书，重点选出莎士比亚的12部经典剧作，在裘克安先生主编的“莎士比亚注释”丛书的基础上进行了改编修订，并加入了精美的插图。裘先生主编的“莎士比亚注释”丛书对莎剧原文做了多方面的详尽注释，对理解原文起到有效作用，在读者中有较广泛的影响。相信这套“莎翁戏剧经典”的出版会进一步推动莎剧在广大读者中的影响力，提高人们对阅读莎剧以及经典文学作品原文的兴趣和能力，产生积极的和广泛的影响。

屠岸 章燕

2013年10月4日

"莎士比亚注释"丛书总序

莎士比亚研究在新中国有过不平坦的道路和坎坷的命运。解放后不久,大家纷纷学俄语,学英语的人数骤减。研究英国文学,要看苏联人怎么说。"文革"十年,莎士比亚同其他西方"资产阶级"作家一样被打入冷宫。改革开放以后,1978 年人民文学出版社出版了在朱生豪译文基础上修订补足的《莎士比亚全集》。随之又出版了一些个别剧的不同译本,如方平译的《莎士比亚喜剧五种》(1979 年)和卞之琳译的《莎士比亚悲剧四种》(1988 年)。梁实秋的译本,现在大陆上也可以读到了。评介和研究莎士比亚的文章,从"文革"结束后才逐渐多起来。

但是,目前多数人学习、欣赏和研究莎士比亚,是通过中译文来进行的。精通英语而研究莎士比亚的学者不是没有,然而他们人数不多,年纪却老迈了。最近若干年,才有一些年轻人到英国或美国去学习和研究莎士比亚。

1981 年我就想到有必要在中国出版我们自己注释的莎士比亚著作。谈起来,许多朋友都赞成。1984 年中国莎士比亚研究会筹备和成立时,我自告奋勇,联系了一些志同道合的学者,共同开始编写莎士比亚注释本。商务印书馆大力支持出版这套丛书。到 2002 年底已出书 26 种,而且第一次印刷版已全部售完。这证明这套丛书是很受欢迎的。

要知道,莎士比亚是英语文学中最优秀的代表人物,他又是英语语言大师,学习、欣赏和研究他的原著,是译文无法替代的。商务印书馆以其远见卓识,早在 1910 年和 1921—1935 年间,就出版过几种莎士比亚剧本的注释本,以满足这方面的需求。那时的教会学校学生英文水平高,能读莎著;不但大学生能读,连有些中学生都能读。可从那时以后,整整 50 年中国就没印过原文的莎士比亚著作。

世界各国,莎著的注释本多得不计其数。如果唯独中国没有,实在说不过去。如果没有,对于中国知识分子欣赏和研究莎士比亚十分不利。近年来,中国人学英语的越来越多了,他们的英文水平也逐渐提高了。因此,也存在着一定的读者市场。

有了注释本,可以为明天的莎士比亚研究提供一个可靠的群众基础。而译本显然不能提供可靠的基础。

莎士比亚是16、17世纪之交的作者,他写的又是诗剧。对于现代的读者,他的英语呈现着不少的困难。不要说掌握了现代英语的中国读者,就是受过一般教育的英美人士,在初读莎士比亚原著时也面临许多障碍,需要注释的帮助。

莎士比亚的时代,英语正从受屈折变化拘束的中世纪英语,向灵活而丰富的现代英语转变。拉丁语和法语当时对英语影响很大。而莎士比亚对英语的运用又有许多革新和创造。主要的困难可以归纳为以下几个方面,也就是注释要提供帮助的方面:

(一)词汇。许多词虽然拼法和现在一样,但具有不同的早期含义,不能望文生义。另有一些词拼法和现在不一样,而含义却相同。莎士比亚独创了一些词。他特别喜欢用双关语,在他创作的早期尤其如此。而双关语是无从翻译的。这是译本无论如何也代替不了注释本的原因之一。

让我们举《哈姆莱特》剧中男主角出场后最初讲的几句话为例:

King:But now,my cousin Hamlet,and my son —
Hamlet〔Aside〕:A little more than kin,and less than kind!
King:How is it that the clouds still hang on you?
Hamlet:Not so,my lord.I am too much i' the sun.

• 梁实秋的译文如下:

王:现在,我的侄子哈姆雷特,也是我的儿子,——
哈[旁白]:比侄子是亲些,可是还算不得儿子。
王:怎么,你脸上还是罩着一层愁云?
哈:不是的,陛下;我受的阳光太多了。

• 卞之琳的译文如下:

王：得，哈姆雷特，我的侄子，我的儿——

哈[旁白]：亲上加亲，越亲越不相亲！

王：你怎么还是让愁云惨雾罩着你？

哈：陛下，太阳大，受不了这个热劲“儿”。

• 朱生豪的译文如下：

王：可是来，我的侄儿哈姆莱特，我的孩子——

哈[旁白]：超乎寻常的亲族，漠不相干的路人。

王：为什么愁云依旧笼罩在你的身上？

哈：不，陛下；我已经在太阳里晒得太久了。

这里，主要困难在于莎士比亚让哈姆莱特使用了 kin 和 kind 以及 son 和 sun 两组双关语。kind 一词又有双关意义，翻译无法完全表达，只能各译一个侧面。结果，梁和卞两先生还得用注释补足其义，朱译则连注释也没有。这种地方，能读原文注释本的人才能充分领略莎氏原意。

哈姆莱特在旁白里说：比亲戚多一点——本来我是你的侄子，现在又成了你的儿子，确实不是一般的亲戚关系啊；然而却比 kind 少一点——kind 有两层意思，一是“同类相求”的亲近感，一是“与人为善”的善意感，我同你没有共同语言，我也不知道你是安的什么心。这话只能对自己说，在舞台上假定对方是听不到的。哈姆莱特的第二句话是公开的俏皮话：哪里有什么阴云呀，我在太阳里晒得不行呢。sun 是跟 clouds 相对；太阳又意味着国王的恩宠，“你对我太好了，我怎么会阴郁呢？”sun 又跟 son 谐音，“做你的儿子，我领教得够了。”原文并不是像梁实秋所说的那样晦涩难解。可是含义太复杂，有隐藏的深层感情，所以无法译得完全。

（二）语法。有些现象，按现代英语语法的标准看，似乎是错误的，但在当时并不错，是属于中世纪英语的残余因素。例如有些动词过去分词的词尾变化、代词的所有格形式、主谓语数的不一致、关系代词和介词的用法等方面，都有一些和现在不同的情况。注释里说明了，可以举一反三去理解。

（三）词序的颠倒和穿插。词尾屈折变化较多的中世纪英语本来对词序没有严格的要求。伊丽莎白时代继承了这种习惯。同时，诗的节律和押韵要求对词序作一定的灵活处理。莎士比亚的舞台语言以鲜明、有力、生动为首要考虑，有时他就把语法和句法放在从属的地位。在激动的台词中，由于思路、感情的变化，语言也常有脱出常规的变化。这些地方，有了注释的指点，理解就容易得多。

（四）典故。莎士比亚用典很多。古希腊、罗马神话，《圣经》故事，英国民间传说，历史逸事……他都随手拈来。其中有一大部分对于英美读者来说乃是常识，但中国读者就很需要注释的帮助。

（五）文化背景。注释可以提供关于基督教义、中世纪传统观点、文艺复兴时期新的主张、英国习俗等方面的知识。

除上述以外，还有莎剧中影射时事，以及版本考据诸问题，在注释本中可以详细论述，也可以简单提及。

世界文豪莫不是语言大师，而要真正理解和欣赏一位大师的文笔，当然非读他的原著不成。出版莎士比亚注释本，首先是为了让中国读者便于买到和读到他的原著。不过我们自知现出的几十种在版本、注释和其他方面还存在不足之处，希望读者多提意见，以便今后不断改进。

裘克安

前　言

《亨利五世》是莎士比亚最著名的英国历史剧，写 1414—1420 年英军以寡敌众战胜法军的故事。它的爱国主义内容在莎士比亚当时英国对抗西班牙的斗争中，以及在第二次世界大战英国反法西斯的斗争中，都起过鼓舞士气的作用，深受英国人民喜爱。

用历史事实写成剧本，通过演出，使人形象地看到哪些历史人物和事件值得褒扬，哪些应予贬斥，并从中接受经验教训，是教育人们的一种有效手段。对于伊丽莎白王朝的英国，这种教育尤其有它的特殊意义。英国从扫帚草王朝（旧译金雀花王朝）的爱德华三世（1327—1377 年在位）起，到都铎王朝的亨利七世（1485—1509 年在位）即位时为止，一百多年中烽烟遍地，战祸连年，断断续续的英法百年战争和持续三十年之久的玫瑰战争给英国人民带来了无穷的灾难。只有到了都铎王朝，国内才出现了相对安定的局面；在女王伊丽莎白时代又击败了西班牙舰队，解除了外来的威胁，从此国势日强，民心振奋。从这些历史事实中人们取得的惨痛教训就是要使国家强盛，人民安宁，首先要有一个权力集中，足以慑服诸侯的王室，其次要有一个英明能干，励精图治的君主。为了普及历史知识，使那些没有受过学校教育，看不懂历史书的人们也能记取这些教训，在伊丽莎白时代的英国舞台上出现了为数不少的历史剧。这些历史剧使人们懂得以往灾难的根源所在，知道今后要追求怎样的理想。在这方面莎士比亚作出了卓越的贡献。他从开始写剧本时对《亨利六世》加以改写起，到他三十五岁时为止（包括据说是和约翰·弗莱切合作写成的《亨利八世》在内），一共写了十个以英王名号为题的剧本，对从理查二世到亨利八世九个英王几乎都已触及。

通过这样系列的介绍，人们对国家兴衰，社会治乱的来龙去脉可以一目了然。

十个英国历史剧中写得尤其出色的当推《亨利四世》上下篇和《亨利五世》。这三个剧本有紧密的内在联系。在前两个剧本中亨利五世还是年轻的哈尔王子，在他的父亲去世后即位为国王，占了较大的篇幅，简直可以说前两个剧本写的就是他的前半生。不过在《亨利四世》上下篇中。莎士比亚为了增添风趣，安插了一个喜剧式的人物福斯泰夫。这个角色的长相滑稽可笑，行为卑鄙无耻，酗酒好色，谎话连篇。要在现实生活中定是个令人望而生厌的家伙；但在舞台上却由于他的插科打诨、幽默风趣，充沛的生活乐趣以及包含真理的老实话，而受到观众的极大欢迎；连伊丽莎白女王看了也赞不绝口，觉得还不过瘾，希望剧作者继续写下去，使莎士比亚欲罢不能。他只好在《亨利四世》下篇的谢幕词中许愿："让约翰爵士（即福斯泰夫）继续登场，还要贡献你们一位有趣的角色，法国的美貌的凯瑟琳公主。"

但在《亨利五世》中莎士比亚没有实现他的诺言的上一半，而是一开始就通过快嘴桂嫂的口述让福斯泰夫在病榻上死去了。这是因为《亨利五世》是一部赞扬亨利五世的丰功伟绩的英雄史诗，一首爱国主义的颂歌；在这样一个庄严肃穆的剧本中，安排几个俯首事敌，卖国求荣的叛徒和几个贪婪无耻，唯利是图的小人，来和英雄人物进行对比，揭示人与人之间的差别，是会起到使主题更鲜明的作用；但要穿插进一个像福斯泰夫那样的笑匠却是不相宜的，那样做会冲淡戏剧的庄严气氛，和剧作者的主要意图格格不入。

根据历史记载，亨利五世在位只有九年。在他短暂的统治期间，最大的历史事件就是和法国的战争。在和勃艮第公爵取得默契的情况下，亨利五世于 1415 年 8 月率兵一万五千人入侵法国，9 月攻下哈弗娄，10 月 25 日被迫与兵力数倍于己的法军决战，取得了阿金考尔战役的大捷。但由于所带兵力有限，不得已撤师回国。当时法军之所以不堪一击，主要是由于内部不团结。法王查理六世患精神病，昏庸无能，由太子掌握政权。和太子争权的还有以阿玛涅克公爵为首和以勃艮第公爵为首的两派。统治阶级内部如此分崩离析，抵御外侮自然软弱无力。亨利五世利用敌人内部纷争的大好时机，于 1417 年再度出征法国，历时三年，至 1419 年底占领了整个诺曼底，迫使法国投降，签订了特洛华和约，承认亨利五世为法国王位继承人，并以法王之女凯瑟琳公主嫁给亨利五世，希冀因王室联姻而永结盟好。

历史剧《亨利五世》的主要情节和霍林谢德史书所载大致不离。不过为了加强戏剧性，莎士比亚往往把时间压缩，加快情节发展。剧中除了一些配角如弗鲁爱林等，历史上没有记载，还有第一幕中法国太子派使者捎来网球对亨利进行嘲弄和讥讽，第三幕中法公主向侍女学英语，以及最终一幕的亨利求婚等场面，可能出自剧作家的巧思虚构以外，其余的人与事大多真实有据。当然，这个剧本主要写的是亨利五世和英法交战，其他人物和事件只能起到陪衬、烘托和对照的作用。剧本对亨利五世的高大形象通过多种表达形式予以充分展示。一开始就由坎特伯雷大主教和伊里主教的交谈对亨利五世即位以后的政绩予以肯定，并把他描绘为一个既有文才武略，又有道德修养，治国有方，深孚众望的圣明君主。随着剧情的发展，他的各种美德也逐渐更充分地显露出来。如在讨论出师法国时他表现得既能深思熟虑，统筹全局，又能敞开思想，博采众议。又如他在几次接见法国使者时，都能待之以礼，有时还犒以重金。即使在盛怒之下也从不失态，充分显示了一国之君应有的豁达大度，饶有政治家风度。在出师之前，先剪除内奸，事先搜集了充分和确凿的证据，但又不露声色，直到适当时机，突然行动，使对方猝不及防，无法狡赖，真是做得干净利索，称得上是胸有成竹，明快果断。他统率军队，纪律严明，对违法乱纪者，一律处以军法，即使对巴道尔夫、尼姆之流，和他曾有交往，也毫不徇情。在强敌当前，身处险境之际，置个人安危于度外，毫无怯懦之色，阿金考尔一役之所以能够取得全胜，多半应归功于他的表率作用。决战前夕，微服出巡，既了解军情，又鼓舞士气。在出巡时他有一段很长的独白，我们可以从中对他的高超的思想境界略窥一二。他身居王位，但视荣华富贵如过眼云烟，一心孜孜不倦为国事操劳。更难能可贵的是毫无骄矜之气，始终保持冷静。在阿金考尔大捷之后，他能考虑到兵力单薄，孤军深入，必遭不测，因此并不乘胜追击，而是毅然决然按原定计划班师回国。就是他向法公主求婚的方式，也别具一格。既不矫揉造作，又不死板生硬，而是动之以情，喻之以理，在温文尔雅中不失刚毅之气，充分表现了好男儿的英雄气概。凡此种种都说明了他是个智勇双全，道德高尚，既能高瞻远瞩，又能洞察一切，有忧国忧民之志，又有任劳任怨之德的贤明君主。他具备了一个理想君主应有的一切品德。无怪人们把他看做英明君主的典型，而把《亨利五世》视为爱国主义的范本。

《亨利五世》中的亨利王和《亨利四世》中的哈尔王子，前后判若两人。从一个玩世不恭，放荡无羁，出没于酒家客店之间，与市井小人为伍，声名狼藉的浪荡王孙公子到一个品格高尚，举止庄重，能文善武，精明强干为众望所归的圣明贤君，中间是有很大的差距的。哈尔王子是怎样逾越这一巨大差距，完成他那奇迹般的转变的？这是一个令人难以理解的问题。如果经过仔细揣摩，我们不难觉察到在他身上具有许多连他的浪荡生活也淹没不了的时而放出异彩的美质。他聪明机智，英勇善战，心地善良，性格开朗，豪爽跌宕，平易近人。他厌恶那些谄媚求宠，阿谀奉承，捏造谣言，搬弄是非的"笑脸的佞人"，因此不愿长期在宫廷里。他痛恨虚伪。他的父王一再现身说法告诫他不要经常在公众场所抛头露面，以使人由于不常见到他而对他产生敬畏。他父亲的说教对他非但不起作用，相反地可能还引起反感。从他即位之后就把理查二世的尸体迁葬威斯敏寺，在决战前夕祈祷上苍不要在这时候记起他父亲的罪过等事看来，他很可能对父王的作为是深感不满的；只是慑于威势，不敢说出罢了。另一方面他年轻时也不是一个胸无大志的人。在《亨利四世》上篇第一幕第二场的结尾，哈尔王子有一段独白很能说明问题。他说："我完全知道你们（指福斯泰夫之流），现在虽然和你们一起无聊鬼混，可是我正在效法太阳，它容忍污浊的浮云遮蔽它的庄严的宝相，然而当它一旦穿破丑恶的雾障，大放光明的时候，人们因为仰望已久，将要格外地惊奇赞叹。”由于他胸怀大志，又具有这些美德，所以他在登基之后，能改弦易辙，一反以往之所为，这是不足为奇的。

《亨利五世》是莎士比亚独力完成的最后一个历史剧，它的首次上演可以确定在1599年4月至6月之间。在写作方法上这个剧本有许多特点。首先，亨利五世两次出征法国，前后共达六年之久；但莎士比亚却只着重地写了阿金考尔战役，对其他有些情节则是通过每一幕前的开场白加以连缀和补充，这样既突出了重点，又照顾到全面，使人既有前后连贯、完整无缺的感觉，又不因平铺直叙、反复重演类似的场面而感到厌倦。而阿金考尔一役也确实富有戏剧性。两军对阵，实力悬殊。英军的精疲力竭和法军的兵强马壮形成了鲜明对比。作战前夕，在英军方面从上到下人人感到岌岌可危，决心殊死一战，而法军方面却是人欢马跃，骄傲轻敌，准备大量抓获俘虏。然而战争结果，却恰恰相反：拥有优势兵力的法军被杀得尸横遍野，一蹶不振，而处于绝对劣势的英军却以微不足道的伤亡换来了全胜。这种戏剧性的大反复会给英国观众带来多大的喜悦是可想而知的。最后，在胜败已成定局之后，亨利五世从法国使者蒙乔的嘴里打听到战场附近的城堡叫阿金考尔，就把那次战役命名为“阿金考尔之役”，这真是道道地地的“画龙点睛”。这些手法都说明了莎士比亚的写作技巧正在日臻完善。在人物塑造方面，莎士比亚也能做到精雕细刻，惟妙惟肖。几乎所有的角色都用自己的语言说话：法国人讲话中很多是法语；快嘴桂嫂喜欢用听人说过但还未弄清涵义的长字眼，弗鲁爱林、麦克摩里斯等不是出生于英格兰本土的人说的英语带有乡土口音，语法错误百出；粗识之无而又好卖弄的毕斯托尔一会儿说上一言半句似通非通的拉丁语，一会儿用上个把西班牙词语，一会儿又七不搭八地把法语作英语来理解；尼姆则是三句不离口头禅，并且一个劲儿地乱用当时流行的字眼；艾丽斯说的英语带有法语腔调；倒是侍童既通英语，又通法语，能替毕斯托尔当翻译，这是由于他原来是由哈尔王子送给福斯泰夫，可能服侍过哈尔王子，受到过一些贵族社会的熏陶和训练。其次从剧中人的说白中可以看出他们的为人。真是闻其声如见其人。譬如桂嫂的心地善良，软弱无能，没有主见；毕斯托尔的卑怯、贪婪，装腔作势，欺软怕硬，一副无赖相；弗鲁爱林的迂腐、固执和民族偏见；以及法国皇太子的轻率浮夸，色厉内荏都跃然纸上，活灵活现。尤其是凯瑟琳公主的形象天真烂漫，伶俐活泼，逗人喜爱。在最末这一点上莎士比亚确实实现了他在《亨利四世》谢幕词中所作出的诺言。

支荩忠

1985 年 4 月于扬州师院

HENRY V

DRAMATIS PERSONAE[1]

KING HENRY[2] THE FIFTH.

DUKE OF GLOSTER, } *brothers to the King.*
DUKE OF BEDFORD, }

DUKE OF EXETER, *uncle to the King.*

DUKE OF YORK, *cousin to the King.*

EARL OF SALISBURY.

EARL OF WESTMORELAND.

EARL OF WARWICK.

ARCHBISHOP OF CANTERBURY.[3]

BISHOP OF ELY.

EARL OF CAMBRIDGE.

LORD SCROOP.

SIR THOMAS GREY.

SIR THOMAS ERPINGHAM, GOWER, FLUELLEN, MACMORRIS, JAMY, *officers in King Henry's army.*

JOHN BATES, ALEXANDER COURT, MICHAEL WILLIAMS, *soldiers in the same.*

PISTOL.

NYM.

BARDOLPH.

BOY.

A HERALD.[4]

CHARLES THE SIXTH, *King of France.*

LOUIS, *the Dauphin.*[5]

DUKE OF BURGUNDY.

DUKE OF ORLEANS.

DUKE OF BOURBON.

THE CONSTABLE OF FRANCE.[6]

RAMBURES, GRANDPRÉ, *Frence Iords.*

GOVERNOR OF HARFLEUR.[7]

MONTJOY, *a French herald.*

AMBASSADORS *to the King of England.*

ISABEL, *Queen of France.*

注　释

1 **Dramatis Personae**〈拉丁语〉：characters of the drama. 剧中人物。

2 人物名字读音：Henry ['henri]，Gloster ['glɔstə]，Bedford ['bedfəd]，Exeter['eksətə]，York[jɔːk]，Salisbury['sɔːlzbəri]，Westmoreland ['westmələnd]，Warwick ['wɔrik]，Ely ['iːli]，Cambridge ['keimbriʤ]，Scroop[skruːpl]，Thomas Grey ['tɔməs grei]，Erpingham ['əːpiŋəm]，Gower['gauə]，Fluellen [flu(ː)'elin]，Macmorris [mæk'mɔːris]，Jamy ['ʤeimi]，John Bates [ʤɔn beitz]，Alexander Court [ælig'zɑːndə kɔːt]，Michael Williams ['maikl 'wiljəmz]，Pistol ['pistl]，Nym [nim]，Bardolph ['bɑːdɔlf]，Charles [ʧɑːlz]，Louis ['luːi]，Burgundy ['bəːgəndi]，Orleans ['ɔːliənz]，Bourbon ['buəbən]，Rambures ['rɔnbjuː]，Grandpré[grôn'pre]，Montjoy[mɔnt'ʤɔi]，Isabel['izəbel]，Katharine ['kæθərin]，Alice ['ælis]，Quickly['kwikli]

3 **Archbishop of Canterbury**：坎特伯雷大主教，是英国教会最高的神职领袖。当时英国教会奉天主教，直属罗马教皇管辖。

4 **herald**：the official messenger of a royal person，传令官。

5 **the Dauphin**：the eldest son of the king of France and the heir to the French throne，法国王子。

6 **Constable**：a principal officer in the royal household，having jurisdiction in matters of arms and chivalry，法国王太子。

7 **Harfleur** [hɑː'fləː]：法国北部海港，当时 Calais 已被英军占领，故 Harfleur 是法方最重要的海港。

KATHARINE, *daughter to Charles and Isabel.*

ALICE, *a lady attending on her.*

HOSTESS *of a tavern in Eastcheap*[8] (*formerly Mistress Quickly*[9], *and now married to Pistol*).

LORDS, LADIES, OFFICERS, SOLDIERS, CITIZENS, MESSENGERS, *and* ATTENDANTS

CHORUS.[10]

SCENE—*England; afterwards France.*

8 Eastcheap [ˈiːstʧiːp]：伦敦城东部一条街。

9 Mistress Quickly：旧时对未婚或已婚妇女都可叫 mistress. 方平译为“快嘴桂嫂”，既取 Quickly 一词之义也取其音。她在《温莎的风流娘儿们》一剧里是仆人。

10 chorus [ˈkɔːrəs]：在古希腊戏剧中是评论剧情的合唱队，在英国戏剧中是开场白和收场白的致辞者。

ACT I PROLOGUE

Enter CHORUS.

CHORUS.

O for a Muse of fire, that would ascend
The brightest heaven of invention, —
A kingdom for a stage, princes to act,
And monarchs to behold the swelling scene!
Then should the warlike Harry, like himself,
Assume the port of Mars; and at his heels,
Leasht-in like hounds, should famine, sword, and fire,
Crouch for employment. But pardon, gentles all,
The flat unraised spirits that have dared
On this unworthy scaffold to bring forth
So great an object: can this cockpit hold
The vasty fields of France? or may we cram
Within this wooden O the very casques
That did affright the air at Agincourt?
O, pardon! since a crookèd figure may
Attest in little place a million;
And let us, ciphers to this great accompt,
On your imaginary forces work.
Suppose within the girdle of these walls
Are now confined two mighty monarchies,
Whose high-uprearèd and abutting fronts
The perilous narrow ocean parts asunder:
Piece out our imperfections with your thoughts;
Into a thousand parts divide one man,
And make imaginary puissance;
Think, when we talk of horses, that you see them
Printing their proud hoofs i'th'receiving earth;—

I. Prologue 第一幕开场白。

1 for：I wish that I had. **Muse**：希腊神话中的女性诗神，有九位。每个诗人有自己的 Muse，指灵感或天才。 **fire**：burning inspiration.欧洲中世纪认为万物由气、火、水、土四种元素构成，其中气和火是轻、亮、上升的元素。 **would**：could. **ascend**：soar to.

2 invention：imagination.

4 swelling：stirring；majestic.

5 warlike：valiant. **Harry**：即亨利五世，他在做王子时期被称 Harry. **like himself**：true to himself.

6 Assume the port：show the bearing or manner. **Mars**：罗马神话中的战神。

7 Leasht-in：一般将三条猎狗拴成一组，叫做 leash，-t 等于-ed. **sword**：喻义 bloodshed，slaughter.

8 Crouch：be ready to spring. **gentles**：gentlefolk.

9 flat unraised：uninspired. **spirits**：actors.

10 unworthy scaffold：crude stage.

11 cockpit：斗鸡场，也曾用作剧场，这里借用来指剧场。

12 vasty：vast.

13 wooden O：木制的圆屋，指剧场。本剧首演在 1599 年 4 月至 6 月，而"环球剧院"是 7 月正式开幕，故这里很可能指"帷幕剧院"，当然后来此剧也在"环球"演过。 **casques**：war helmets.

14 affright：frighten. **Agincourt**['æʤinkɔːt]：法国地名，1415 年 10 月 25 日亨利五世在这里打败法国军队。见本剧第 4 幕。

15 a crookèd figure：a curved cipher，指 0，谓 100,000 添一个 0 就变成 1,000,000。figure 还有"人物"的双关义，谓舞台上一个兵可能代表百万兵。

16 Attest：represent.

17 accompt：account，①总数；②叙述。

18 On…work：work on your imagination.

19 girdle：circumference. **these walls**：the walls of the playhouse.

20 two mighty monarchies：referring to the kingdoms of England and France.

21 high-uprearèd：rearing high，lofty. **abutting**：projecting toward each other. **fronts**：the cliffs of dover（英岸）and Calais（法岸）。

22 perilous narrow ocean：the English Channel.整句核心部分为 The ocean parts asunder the fronts of the two monarchies.

23 Piece out：eke out；augment.

25 puissance：strength.

27 i'th'：in the，省略字母时用 apostrophe 代替，目的为减少音节。（下同时，不再注释） **receiving**：soft and yielding，easy to be imprinted.

For 'tis your thoughts that now must deck our kings,
Carry them here and there; jumping o'er times,
Turning th' accomplishment of many years
Into an hour-glass; for the which supply,
Admit me Chorus to this history;
Who, prologue-like, your humble patience pray,
Gently to hear, kindly to judge, our play. [*Exit*.

28 **deck**：dress up；adorn.

29 **times**：periods of time.

30—31 **Turning … hour-glass**：crowding the happenings of years into an hour. **hour-glass**：玻璃的沙漏计时器，一般为一小时漏完。按本剧演 1414 年到 1420 年共六年余的史事，演剧大约只用两小时。

31 **for the which supply**：for the supply of which，i.e. for filling up the intervals in the action — the periods over which we have to jump.

32 **me**：Chorus 的同位语。 **history**：historical play.

33 **Who**：指 me，谓语 pray.

ACT I

SCENE I

London. An ante-chamber in the KING'S *palace.*

Enter the ARCHBISHOP OF CANTERBURY
and the BISHOP OF ELY.

ARCHBISHOP OF CANTERBURY.

My lord, I'll tell you, —that self bill is urged,
Which in th' eleventh year of the last king's reign
Was like, and had indeed against us past,
But that the scambling and unquiet time
Did push it out of further question.

BISHOP OF ELY.

But how, my lord, shall we resist it now?

ARCHBISHOP OF CANTERBURY.

It must be thought on. If it pass against us,
We lose the better half of our possession;
For all the temporal lands, which men devout
By testament have given to the church,
Would they strip from us; being valued thus,—
As much as would maintain, to the king's honor,
Full fifteen earls and fifteen hundred knights,
Six thousand and two hundred good esquires;
And, to relief of lazas and weak age,
Of indigent faint souls past corporal toil,
A hundred almshouses right well supplied;
And to the coffers of the king, beside,
A thousand pounds by th' year: thus runs the bill.

BISHOP OF ELY.

I.i（第一幕第一场，后类推）（以下黑体数字为行码）

1 **self**：same. **bill**：指 Lollards 派贵族在国会提出的要求剥夺天主教会财产的法案。Lollards 为追随或接近 Wycliffe 教义的早期新教派。 **urged**：put forward for consideration.

2 **last king**：Henry IV，他在位第 11 年是 1410 年，即第一场的四年前。

3 **Was like**：was likely（to be passed）. **had … against us past**：would have been passed despite our opposition.

4 **But that**：but for the fact that，若不是。 **scambling**：turbulent.

5 **question**：consideration，审议。

8 **the better half**：the larger half.

9 **temporal lands**：estates not originally belonging to the church. **men devout**：形容词在其修饰的名词之后，系受法语影响。

10 **testament**：遗嘱。

11 **strip**：take away. **valued**：estimated.

12 **As much as would**：enough to. **maintain**：support. **to the king's honor**：to bring honor to the king.

14 **esquires**：men belonging to the higher order of English gentry，ranking immediately below knights.

15 **lazas**：poor and diseased people，esp. lepers.

16 **indigent faint souls**：needy and feeble men. **past**：已不能从事。 **corporal toil**：physical labor.

17 **right**：very.

18 **coffers**：treasury. **beside**：besides.

19 **by th' year**：every year. **runs**：says.

This would drink deep.

ABCHBISHOP OF CANTERBURY.

'Twould drink the cup and all.

BISHOP OF ELY.

But what prevention?

ARCHBISHOP OF CANTERBURY.

The king is full of grace and fair regard.

BISHOP OF ELY.

And a true lover of the holy church.

ARCHBISHOP OF CANTERBURY.

The courses of his youth promised it not.
The breath no sooner left his father's body,
But that his wildness, mortified in him,
Seem'd to die too; yea, at that very moment,
Consideration, like an angel, came,
And whipt th' offending Adam out of him,
Leaving his body as a paradise,
T' envelop and contain celestial spirits.
Never was such a sudden scholar made;
Never came reformation in a flood.
with such a heady currance, scouring faults;
Nor never Hydra-headed wilfulness
So soon did lose his seat, and all at once,
As in this king.

BISHOP OF ELY.

We are blessed in the change.

ARCHBISHOP OF CANTERBURY.

Hear him but reason in divinity,
And, all-admiring, with an inward wish
You would desire the king were made a prelate:
Hear him debate of commonwealth affairs,
You would say it hath been all-in-all his study:
List his discourse of war, and you shall hear
A fearful battle render'd you in music:

20 drink deep：drain (our resources).

21 drink the cup and all：make us quite destitute.

22 what prevention?：what must be done to prevent this.

23 grace：神恩。史称亨利五世在年轻时生活放荡，在父病死之际他突蒙神恩，变得虔诚，改恶从善。 **regard**：intention；design.

25 courses：habits；way of life. **promised**：predicted；foretold.

26—27 no sooner…But that：no sooner…than. **mortified**：destrouyed；killed.按天主教教义，在神恩冲击下，原罪的旧我死去，信徒获得新生。

28 yea：yes.

29 Consideration：spiritual self-examination.

30 offending Adam：人类始祖亚当违背神命，被赶出天堂，见《圣经·旧约·创世记》第 3 章。

33 scholar：中世纪的学者，首先是个神学家。

35 heady：headlong；impetuous. **currance**：current. **scouring**：cleansing.

36 Hydra[ˈhaidrə]：希腊神话中多头的妖蛇，它的一个头被刀砍掉，立刻会长出两个头。

37 his：its，of 'wilfulness'. **seat**：throne；dominant position.

38 As：和 32 行以及 34 行中的 such 以及 36 行中的 so 互相呼应。

39 Hear him but reason in：if you only hear him discuss. **divinity**：theology.

40 all-admiring：admiring everything he says.

41 You would desire：后省略连词 that. **were made a prelate**：should be made a bishop.

42 debate of：discuss. **commonwealth affairs**：public affairs.

43 all-in-all his study：his only study.

44 List：listen to.

45 render'd you：depicted to you.

Turn him to any cause of policy,
The gordian knot of it he will unloose,
Familiar as his garter:—that, when he speaks,
The air, a charter'd libertine, is still,
And the mute wonder lurketh in men's ears,
To steal his sweet and honey'd sentences;
So that the art and practic part of life
Must be the mistress to this theoric:
Which is a wonder how his Grace should glean it,
Since his addiction was to courses vain;
His companies unletter'd, rude, and shallow;
His hours fill'd up with riots, banquets, sports;
And never noted in him any study,
Any retirement, any sequestration
From open haunts and popularity.

BISHOP OF ELY.

The strawberry grows underneath the nettle,
And wholesome berries thrive and ripen best
Neighbor'd by fruit of baser quality:
And so the prince obscured his contemplation
Under the veil of wildness; which, no doubt,
Grew like the summer grass, fastest by night,
Unseen, yet crescive in his faculty.

ARCHBISHOP OF CANTERBURY.

It must be so; for miracles are ceased;
And therefore we must needs admit the means
How things are perfected.

BISHOP OF ELY.

But, my good lord.
How now for mitigation of this bill
Urged by the commons? Doth his majesty
Incline to it, or no?

ARCHBISHOP OF CANTERBURY.

He seems indifferent;

46 **Turn him to**: turn his attention to. **cause of policy**: problem of state.

47 **gordian knot**: 希腊传说中 Phrygian King Gordius 打的一个结,无人能解开。

48 **garter**: 袜带。 **that**: so that.

49 **charter'd libertine**: free spirit licensed to go where it wishes. **still**: 静止。

50 这里把 wonder 拟人化了。

52 **So that**: from this we may conclude that. **art and practic part**: practical skill and experience.

53 **be the mistress to**: govern. **theoric**: theoretical knowledge.

54 **his Grace**: 指 Henry V,相当于陛下。

55 **addiction**: inclination; bent. **courses**: 见 24 行。 **vain**: worthless.

56 **companies**: companions. **rude**: coarse.

59 **sequestration**: seclusion.

60 **open haunts**: places of common resort. **popularity**: mixing with common people.

61 **grows**: grows well.

64 **obscured**: hid. **contemplation**: religious meditation.

65 **which**: 指 contemplation.

67 **crescive**: increasing. **his faculty**: its (contemplation's) natural capacity.

68 **ceased**: no more.

69 **admit**: accept.

70 **How**: by which.

72 **mitigation**: making less harmful.

75 **indifferent**: impartial.

Or, rather, swaying more upon our part
Than cherishing th' exhibiters against us:
For I have made an offer to his majesty,—
Upon our spiritual convocation,
And in regard of causes now in hand,
Which I have open'd to his Grace at large,
As touching France,—to give a grater sum
Than ever at one time the clergy yet
Did to his predecessors part withal.

BISHOP OF ELY.

How did this offer seem received, my lord?

ARCHBISHOP OF CANTERBURY.

With good acceptance of his majesty;
Save that there was not time enough to hear —
As, I perceived, his grace would fain have done —
The severals and unhidden passages
Of his true titles to some certain dukedoms,
And, generally, to the crown and seat of France,
Derived from Edward, his great-grandfather.

BISHOP OF ELY.

What was th' impediment that broke this off?

ARCHBISHOP OF CANTERBURY.

The French ambassador upon that instant
Craved audience;—and the hour, I think, is come
To give him hearing: is it four o'clock?

BISHOP OF ELY.

It is.

ARCHBISHOP OF CANTERBURY.

Then go we in, to know his embassy;
Which I could, with a ready guess, declare,
Before the Frenchman speak a word of it.

BISHOP OF ELY.

I'll wait upon you; and I long to hear it. [*Exeunt*.

80 **swaying more upon our part**：inclining our way.

81 **cherishing**：favoring. **exhibiters**：proposers of the bill in parliament.

83 **Upon**：in accordance with. **spiritual convocation**：a meeting of the religious heads.

84 **causes**：issues.

85 **open'd**：revealed；explained. **at large**：fully.

86 **As touching**：regarding，说明前面 causes，从 Upon 到 France 为插入语。

88 **Did…part withal**：gave.

90 It has been received well by his Majesty.

91 **Save**：except；only.

92 **As**：which (meaning 'to hear').

93 **severals**：details. **unhidden passages**：clear lines of succession.

94 **titles**：所有权，继承权。

95 **seat**：throne.

96 **Edward**：Edward III，亨利五世的曾祖父，他的母亲是法国菲利普四世之女伊莎贝拉。

97 What happened to prevent him from hearing you out?

102 **embassy**：mission.

105 **wait upon**：accompany.

SCENE II

The same. The Presence-chamber.

Enter KING HENRY, GLOSTER, BEDFORD, EXETER, WARWICK, WESTMORELAND, *and* ATTENDANTS.

KING HENRY.

Where is my gracious Lord of Canterbury?

DUKE OF EXETER.

Not here in presence.

KING HENRY.

Send for him, good uncle.

EARL OF WESTMORELAND.

Shall we call in th' ambassador, my liege?

KING HENRY.

Not yet, my cousin: we would be resolved,
Before we hear him, of some things of weight,
The task our thoughts, concerning us and France.

Enter the ARCHBISHOP OF CANTERBURY *and the* BISHOP OF ELY.

ARCHBISHOP OF CANTERBURY.

God and his angels guard your sacred throne,
And make you long become it!

KING HENRY.

Sure, we thank you.
My learned lord, we pray you to proceed,
And justly and religiously unfold
Why the law Salique, that they have in France,
Or should, or should not, bar us in our claim:
And God forbid, my dear and faithful lord.
That you should fashion, wrest, or bow your reading.
Or nicely charge your understanding soul
With opening titles miscreate, whose right
Suits not in native colors with the truth;

I.ii

1 **Lord of Canterbury**：即 Archbishop of Canterbury.

2 **uncle**：Duke of Exeter was half-brother of Henry IV，Henry V's father.

3 **liege**：sovereign lord.

4 **cousin**：一般的亲属都可叫 cousin. **we**：royal we，国王自称，相当于“朕”。 **be resolved**：come to a decision.

5 **weight**：importance.

6 **task**：occupy fully.

8 **become**：adorn；grace.

10 **unfold**：reveal；bring to light.

11 **the law Salique**：中世纪日耳曼法兰克人的一支萨利族的法律，其中有妇女不得继承王位的规定。这法律为法国所采用。

12 **Or…，or**：either…or. **claim**：对继承法国王位的权利要求。

14 **fashion**：counterfeit. **wrest**：distort. **bow**：cause to bend. **reading**：interpretation.

15 **nicely … soul**：sophistically burden your soul with guilt by knowingly misrepresenting the case.

16 **opening**：revealing；disclosing. **miscreate**：illegitimate. **whose**：指 titles，见上场 87 行。

17 **Suits not**：does not match. **in native colors**：if not distorted；in essence.

For God doth know how many, now in health,
Shall drop their blood in approbation
Of what your reverence shall incite us to.
Therefore take heed how you impawn our person,
How you awake the sleeping sword of war!
We charge you, in the name of God, take heed;
For never two such knigdoms did contend
Without much fall of blood; whose guiltless drops
Are every one a woe, a sore complaint
'Gainst him whose wrongs gives edge unto the swords
That make such waste in brief mortality.
Under this conjuration, speak, my lord;
For we will hear, note, and believe in heart
That what you speak is in your conscience washt
As pure as sin with baptism.

ARCHBISHOP OF CANTERBURY.

Then hear me, gracious sovereign,—and you peers,
That owe yourselves, your lives, and services
To this imperial throne.—There is no bar
To make against your highness' claim to France
But this, which they produce from Pharamond,—
In terram Salicam mulieres ne succedant,
'No woman shall succeed in Salique land:'
Which Salique land the French unjustly gloze
To be the realm of France, and Pharamond
The founder of this law and female bar.
Yet their own authors faithfully affirm
That the land Salique is in Germany,
Between the floods of Sala and of Elbe;
Where Charles the Great, having subdued the Saxons,
There left behind and settled certain French;
Who, holding in disdain the German women
For some dishonest manners of their life,
Establisht then this law,—to wit, no female

18 **God doth know**：only God knows.

19 **drop**：shed. **in approbation**：in proving.

20 **your reverence**：对大主教的尊称。 **incite**：induce，注意此字当时没有现代“挑唆”这样的贬义。

21 **impawn**：pledge；commit.

25 **fall**：shedding. **guiltless**：innocent.

26 **woe**：grievance.

27 **'Gainst**：against. **wrongs**：wrong-doings，复数主语用单数谓语。 **gives edge unto the swords**：start the war.

28 **mortality**：life (lives) of men.

32 **baptism**：洗礼。基督教认为受洗礼即洗去原罪，洗礼一般由教士对婴儿施行，以后也有成人受洗礼的。

33 **peers**：lords，贵族。

35 **bar**：obstacle.

37 **But**：except. **Pharamond**：传说中萨利族的王。

38 拉丁文，39 行为英译文。

40 **gloze**：interpret.

41 **Pharamond**：后省略 to be.

42 **female bar**：restriction against women.

45 **floods**：rivers.

46 **Charles the Great**：Charlemagne，查理曼大帝（768—814 A.D. 为法兰克王，800 A.D.被教皇封为神圣罗马皇帝）。

49 **dishonest manners**：immoral conduct.

50 **to wit**：that is to say.

Should be inheritrix in Salique land:
Which Salique, as I said, 'twixt Elbe and Sala,
Is at this day in Germany call'd Meisen.
Then doth it well appear, the Salique law
Was not devised for the realm of France:
Nor did the French possess the Salique land
Until four hundred one and twenty years
After defunction of King Pharamond,
Idly supposed the founder of this law;
Who died within the year of our redemption
Four hundred twenty-six; and Charles the Great
Subdued the Saxons, and did seat the French
Beyond the river Sala, in the year
Eight hundred five. Besides, their writers say,
King Pepin, which deposed Childeric,
Did, as heir general, being descended
Of Blithild, which was daughter to King Clothair,
Make claim and title to the crown of France.
Hugh Capet also,—who usurpt the crown
Of Charles the duke of Lorraine, sole heir male
Of the true line and stock of Charles the Great,—
To find his title with some shows of truth,
Though, in pure truth, it was corrupt and naught,
Convety'd himself as heir to th' Lady Lingare,
Daughter to Charlemain, who was the son
To Louis the emperor, and Louis the son
Of Charles the Great. Also King Louis the Tenth,
Who was sole heir to the usurper Capet,
Could not keep quiet in his conscience,
Wearing the crown of France, till satisfied
That fair Queen Isabel, his grandmother,
Was lineal of the Lady Ermengare,
Daughter to Charles the foresaid duke of Lorraine:
By the which marriage the line of Charles the Great

52 'twixt：between.

53 Meisen：现拼法为 Meissen['maisən]

58 defunction：death.

59 Idly：foolishly.supposed 后省略 to be.

60 year of our redemption：我们得救年，也就是耶稣诞生年，即西历纪元。基督教认为上帝派耶稣下凡，是为了拯救世人。

62 seat：settle.

64 their：French.

65 King Pepin：加洛林王朝始祖，752—768 在位。 **which**：who. **Childeric**（Childeric III）：梅罗文加王朝的末代国王，743—752 在位。

66 heir general：descendent.

67 Of：from. **King Clothair**（Clothair I）：法兰克国王，511—561 在位。

69 Hugh Capet：法兰西国王，987—996 在位。谓语为 74 行的 conveyed. **usurpt**：usurped.

72 To find：in order to provide. **shows**：appearance，伊丽莎白时期，抽象名词可加 s.

73 it：指上一行中的 title. **corrupt and naught**：illegal and invalid.

74 Convey'd himself：passed himself off. **Lingare**：Lingard.

75 Charlemain：应为 Charles the Bald，查理曼的孙子，法兰西国王，843—877 在位，同时为神圣罗马皇帝，称号为 Charles II，875—877 在位。莎士比亚跟着历史学家霍林谢德弄错了名字。

76 Louis the emperor：查理曼大帝之子，778—840 为神圣罗马皇帝，814—840 同时为法兰克国王。

77 Louis the Tenth：应为 Louis the Ninth，也称圣路易，法兰西国王，1226—1270 在位。莎士比亚跟着历史学家霍林谢德弄错了名字。

82 lineal of：directily descended from. **Ermengare**：Ermengard.

84 the which：which.

Was re-united to the crown of France.
so that, as clear as is the summer's sun,
King Pepin's title, and Hugh Capet's claim,
King Louis his satisfaction, all appear
To hold in right and title of the female:
So do the kings of France unto this day;
Howbeit they would hold up this Salique law
To bar your highness claiming from the female;
And rather choose to hide them in a net
Than amply to imbar their crooked titles
Usurpt from you and your progenitors.

KING HENRY.

May I with right and conscience make this claim?

ARCHBISHOP OF CANTERRURY.

The sin upon my head, dread sovereign!
For in the Book of Numbers is it writ,—
When the man dies, let the inheritance
Descend unto the daughter. Gracious lord,
Stand for your own; unwind your bloody flag;
Look back into your mighty ancestors:
Go, my dread Lord, to your great-grandsire's tomb,
From whom you claim; invoke his warlike spirit,
And your great-uncle's, Edward the Black Prince,
Who on the French ground play'd a tragedy,
Making defeat on the full power of France,
Whiles his most mighty father on a hill
Stood smiling to behold his lion's whelp
Forage in bllod of French nobility.
O noble English, that could entertain
With half their forces the full pride of France,
And let another half stand laughing by,
All out of work and cold for action!

BISHOP OF ELY.

Awake remembrance of these valiant dead,
And with your puissant arm renew their feats:

88 **King Louis his satisfaction**：King Louis' satisfaction (about his possession of the French crown having some appearance of legitimacy). 以 s 结尾的人名的所有格，用加 his 表达，不用 apostrophe，这是伊丽莎白时期的做法。 **appear**：are clearly seen.

89 **To hold**：to be valid. **in right**：in the right.

90 **unto**：to.

91 **Howbeit**：however. **hold up**：maintain.

92 **highness**：后面省略 apostrophe.

93 **hide them in a net**：take refuge behind a flimsy pretext (the Salique law).

94 **imbar**：fence around. 有些考据者认为此字应为 imbare，解为 reveal to view.

97 **The sin upon my head**：If I commit the sin of deceiving you, let me be punished (upon one's head：由……负责). **dread**：dreaded; revered.

98 **Book of Numbers**：《圣经·旧约·民数记》第 27 章 8 节："If a man die, and have no son, then ye shall cause his inheritance to pass unto his daughter…". **writ**：written.

101 **Stand for**：stand up for; rise in defense of. **unwind** [ˌʌnˈwaind]：unfurl. **bloody**：blood-red.

103 **great-grandsire's**：Edward III's，见 89 行。

104 **From whom you claim**：on whose right you base your claim to the French crown.

105 And that of your great-uncle, Edward the Black Prince.

106 **tragedy**：the Battle of Crécy (1346).

107 **Making**：inflicting.

108 **Whiles**：while.

111 **entertain**：handle, engage (an enemy).

112 **pride**：company of troops.

114 **cold for action**：feeling cold for lack of action.

116 **puissant**：powerful.

You are their heir ; you sit upon their throne;
The blood and courage that renownèd them
Runs in your veins; and my thrice-puissant liege
Is in the very May-morn of his youth,
Ripe for exploits and mighty enterprises.

DUKE OF EXETER.

Your brother kings and monarchs of the earth
Do all expect that you should rouse yourself,
As did the former lions of your blood.

EARL OF WESTMORELAND.

They know your Grace hath cause and means and might;
So hath your highness; never king of England
Had nobles richer and more loyal subjects,
Whose hearts have left their bodies here in England,
And lie pavilion'd in the fields of France.

ARCHBISHOP OF CANTERBURY.

O, let their bodies follow, my dear liege,
With blood and sword and fire to win your right:
In aid whereof we of the spirituality
Will raise your highness such a mighty sum
As never did the clergy at one time
Bring in to any of your ancestors.

KING HENRY.

We must not only arm t' invade the French,
But lay down our proportions to defend
Against the Scot, who will make road upon us
With all advantages.

ARCHBISHOP OF CANTERBURY.

They of those marches, gracious sovereigh,
Shall be a wall sufficient to defend
Our inland from the pilfering borderers.

KING HENRY.

We do not mean the coursing snatchers only,
But fear the main intendment of the Scot,

118 **renownèd**: made famous.

119 **thrice-puissant**: that is, mighty in his own right and preceded by two mighty ancestors (Edward III and Edward the Balck Prince).

120 **May-morn**: prime 20 到 35 岁，当时 Henry V 为 27 岁。

126—127 **never king… subjects**: Never had a king of England richer nobles and more loyal subjects than you have.

129 **pavilion'd**: in their tents.

132 **whereof**: of which(your right). **spirituality**: clergy.

134 **at one time**: at any other time.

137 **lay down**: formulate. **proportions**: estimate of forces and supplies required.

138 **road**: inroad; raid.

140 **They**: the men. **marches**: borders.

143 **coursing**: marauding. **snatchers**: freebooters.

144 **intendment**: intent; design.

Who hath been still a giddy neighbor to us;
For you shall read that my great-grandfather
Never went with his forces into France,
But that the Scot on his unfurnisht kingdom
Came pouring, like the tide into a breach,
With ample and brim fulness of his force;
Galling the gleanèd land with hot assays,
Girding with grievous siege castles and towns;
That England, being empty of defence,
Hath shook and trembled at th' ill neighborhood.

ARCHBISHOP OF CANTERBURY.

She hath been then more fear'd that harm'd, my liege
For hear her but exampled by herself:—
When all her chivalry hath been in France,
And she a mourning widow of her nobles,
She hath herself not only well defended
But taken, and impounded as a stray,
The King of Scots; whom she did send to France,
To fill King Edward's fame with prisoner kings,
And make her chronicle as rich with praise
As is the ooze and bottom of the sea
With sunken wrack and sumless treasuries.

EARL OF WESTMORELAND.

But there's a saying, very old and true,—
'If that you will France win,'
Then with Scothland first begin:
For once the eagle England being in prey,
To her unguarded nest the weasel Scot
Comes sneaking, and so sucks her princely eggs;
Playing the mouse in absence of the cat,
To spoil and havoc more that she can eat.

DUKE OF EXETER.

It follows, then, the cat must stay at home:
Yet that is but a curst necessity,

145 **still**：constantly；always. **giddy**：unstable.

146 **read**：learn from history books.

148 **unfurnisht**：defenseless；unprotected.

150 **brim fulness**：condition of being full to the brim.

151 **gleanèd**：stripped (of defenders). **assays**：forays；attacks.

152 **grievous**：causing grief and suffering.

153 **That**：so that.

154 **shook**：shaken. **ill**：morally evil；wicked.

155 **She**：England. **fear'd**：frightened.

156 For note only the examples (precedents) she has set for herself.

157 **chivalry**：men-at-arms.

160 **impounded**：held in jail. **stray**：animal found wandering out of bound.

161 **King of Scots**：David II, who was taken prisoner at the Battle of Neville's Cross (1346) duringt Edward III's absence in France.

162 **fill**：enlarge；aggrandize.

163 **her**：England's.

165 **wrack**：wrecked ships. **sumless**：incalculable.

167 **If that**：if.

169 **in prey**：in search of prey.

173 **havoc**：damage.

175 **curst** (crushed)：forced；strained.勉强的。

Since we have locks to safeguard necessaries,
And pretty traps to catch the petty thieves.
While that the armed hand doth fight abroad,
Th' advisèd head defends itself at home;
For government, though high, and low, and lower,
Put into parts, doth keep in one concent,
Congreeing in a full and natural close,
Like music.

ARCHBISHOP OF CANTERBURY.

True: therefore doth heaven divide
The state of man in divers functions,
Setting endeavor in continual motion;
To which is fixed, as an aim or butt,
Obedience: for so work the honey-bees,
Creatures that, by a rule in nature, teach
The act of order to a peopled kingdom.
They have a king, and officers of sorts:
Where some, like magistrates, correct at home;
Others, like merchants, venture trade abroad;
Others, like soldiers, armed in their stings,
Make boot upon the summer's velvet buds;
Which pillage they with merry march bring home
To the tent-royal of their emperor:
Who, busied in his majesty, surveys
The singing masons building roofs of gold;
The civil citizens kneading-up the honey;
The poor mechanic porters crowding in
Their leavy burdens at his narrow gate;
The sad-eyed justice, with his surly hum,
Delivering o'er to executors pale
The lazy yawning drone. I this infer,—
That many things, having full reference
To one concent, may work contrariously:
As many arrows, loosed several ways,

177 pretty: cleverly-devised; skilfully made.

178 While that: while.

179 Th' advisèd: the judicious.

181 Put into parts: divided among the various heads of state, as are the various parts of music among the players. **concent**: consent; harmony.

182 Congreeing: harmonizing. **close**: cadence,结尾的旋律。

184 The state of man: man looked upon as a state in miniature, a body politic.

186 butt: target.

184—187 The state … Obedience: Therefore (to secure this harmony) heaven assigns to the members their different functions, to the exercise of which they are continually prompted, and these functions are directed at the common aim — obedience.

188 rule: law.

189 The act of order: orderly action. **peopled kingdom**: human society.

190 of sorts: of various ranks.

191 correct: set things in order.

192 venture: dare to carry on.

194 Make boot upon: plunder.

195 pillage: booty.

197 busied in his majesty: occupied with his royal responsibilities. **surveys**: oversees; supervises.

199 civil: well-governed; orderly.

200 mechanic: engaged in manual occupation. **crowding in**: bringing in a crowd.

202 sad-eyed: grave-looking.

203 executors: executioners.

205 reference: relation.

206 To one concent: towards one aim.

207 loosed several ways: shot from different directions.

Fly to one mark;
As many several ways meet in one town;
As many fresh streams run in opne self sea;
As many lines close in the dial's center;
So may a thousand actions, once afoot,
End in one purpose, and be all well borne
Without defeat. Therefore to France, my liege.
Divide your happy England into four;
Whereof take you one quarter into France,
And you withal shall make all Gallia shake.
If we, with thrice such powers left at home,
Cannot defend our own doors from the dog,
Let us be worried, and our nation lose
The name of hardiness and policy.

KING HENRY.

Call in the messengers sent from the Dauphin.

[*Exeunt some* ATTENDANTS.]

Now are we well resolved; and, by God's help,
And yours, the noble sinews of our power,
France being ours, we 'll bend it to our awe,
Or break it all to pieces: or there we 'll sit,
Ruling in large and ample empery
O'er France and all her almost kingly dukedoms,
Or lay these bones in an unworthy urn,
Tombless, with no remembrance over them:
Either our history shall with full mouth
Speak freely of our acts, or else our grave,
Like Turkish mute, shall have a tongueless mouth,
Not worshipt with a waxen epitaph.

Enter AMBASSADORS *of France*, *attended*.

Now are we well prepared to know the pleasure
Of our fair cousin Dauphin; for we hear
Your greeting is from him, not from the king.

FIRST AMBASSADOR.

211 **close**：meet. **dial's**：sundial's.

213 **borne**：carried out.

217 **withal**：with it. **Gallia**：Gaul (France).

218 **powers**：forces.

220 **worried**：savaged (as by a dog).

221 **policy**：wisdom in affairs of state.

222 **Dauphin**['dɔːfin]：法国王太子，查理六世长子，名 Louis，或作 Lewis.

223 **we**：royal we.

225 **ours**：our rightful possession. **bend**：subdue.

227 **empery**：absolute dominion.

230 **remembrance**：memorial inscription.

233 **mute**：古代土耳其有些罪犯被割舌，不能讲话。

234 **with a waxen epitaph**：even with a perishable memorial.

235 **pleasure**：will；desire.

236 **cousin**：a word used by a sovereign or nobleman to call another.

237 **king**：法国国王查理六世，1380—1422 在位。但他 1392 年得热病伤脑，患精神病，实际成为傀儡。因他是英女王伊丽莎白一世的祖先，莎士比亚讳言他的这种病。

May 't please your majesty to give us leave
Freely to render what we have in charge;
Or shall we sparingly show you far off
The Dauphin's meaning and our embassy?

KING HENRY.

We are no tyrant, but a Christian king;
Unto whose grace our passion is as subject
As are our wretches fetter'd in our prisons:
Therefore with frank and with uncurbed plainness
Tell us the Dauphin's mind.

FIRST AMBASSADOR.

Thus, then, in few.
Your highness, lately sending into France,
Did claim some certain dukedoms, in the right
Of your great predecessor, King Edward the Third.
In answer of which claim, the prince our master
Says, that you savor too much of your youth;
And bids you be advised, there 's naught in France
That can be with a nimble galliard won; —
You cannot revel into dukedoms there.
He therefore sends you, meeter for your spirit,
This tun of treasure; and, in lieu of this,
Desires you let the dukedoms that you claim
Hear no more of you. This the Dauphin speaks.

KING HENRY.

What treasure, uncle?

DUKE OF EXETER.

Tennis-balls, my liege.

KING HENRY.

We are glad the Dauphin is so pleasant with us:
His present and your pains we thank you for:
When we have matcht our rackets to these balls,
We will, in France, by God's grace, play a set
Shall strike his father's crown into the hazard.

238 **May 't**: may it. **leave**: permission.

239 **Freely**: without restraint. **what we have in charge**: what we have been entrusted to convey.

240 **off**: departing from.

243 **grace**: spiritual virtue (of a christian king). **subject**: obedient.

246 **in few**: in a few words.

251 **savor … of**: suggest by taste, smell or manner the presence of.

252 **advised**: informed. **naught**: nothing.

253 **galliard**: a lively French dance.

255 **meeter**: more suitable.

256 **tun**: keg; barrel.

260 **pleasant**: jocular; merry.

261 **pains**: trouble.

262 **matcht**: matched, got used.

263 **set**: set of tennis,后面省略 that.

264 **hazard**: 旧时室内网球场内圈墙上的缺口叫 hazards,把球打入这种缺口可得分。

Tell him he hath made a match with such a wrangler
That all the courts of France will be disturb'd
With chases. And we understand him well,
How he comes o'er us with our wilder days,
Not measuring what use we made of them.
We never valued this poor seat of England;
And therefore, living hence, did give ourself
To barbarous licence; as 'tis ever common
That men are merriest when they are from home.
But tell the Dauphin, I will keep my state,
Be like a king, and show my sail of greatness,
When I do rouse me in my throne of France:
For that I have laid by my majesty,
And plodded like a man for working-days;
But I will rise there with so full a glory,
That I will dazzle all the eyes of France,
Yea, strike the Dauphin blind to look on us.
And tell the pleasant prince, this mock of his
Hath turn'd his balls to gun-stones, and his soul
Shall stand sore chargèd for the wasteful vengeance
That shall fly with them: for many a thousand widows
Shall this his mock mock out of their dear husbands;
Mock mothers from their sons, mock castles down;
And some are yet ungotten and unborn
That shall have cause to carse the Dauphin's scorn.
But this lies all within the will of God,
To whom I do appeal; and in whose name,
Tell you the Dauphin, I am coming on,
To venge me as I may, and to put forth
My rightful hand in a well-hallow'd cause.
So, get you hence in peace; and tell the Dauphin,
His jest will savor but of shallow wit,
When thousands weep, more than did laugh at it.—
Convey them with safe conduct.—Fare you well.

265 **wrangler**：opponent；contestant.

266 **courts**：①网球场；②宫廷。

267 **chases**：旧时室内网球赛中球着地两次接不起即失分，叫 chases.

268 **comes o'er us with**：reminds me of；seeks to belittle me with. **wilder days**：指 Henry V 年轻为王子时期的一段放荡生活，参见莎士比亚《亨利四世》上下篇。

269 **measuring**：judging.

270 **seat**：throne.

271 **hence**：away from here (the court of England).

272 **barbarous**：coarse.

273 **from**：away from.

274 **state**：royal dignity.

275 **sail**：full swell.

277 **For that**：for. **laid by**：put aside.

278 **plodded**：toiled；drudged. **man for working-days**：day laborer.

279 **there**：in my throne of France.这里自喻为太阳。

282 **pleasant**：见 260 行。

283 **gun-stones**：cannon-balls.

284 **sore chargèd**：grievously burdened with responsibility.

285 **them**：gun-stones.

286 his mock will mock（临时作动词 pull 讲，下同）widows out of their husbands.

288 **ungotten**：unbegotten.

293 **venge me**：avenge myself.

295 **get you hence**：go away.

298 **Convey them with safe conduct**：escort them away in safety，这句话对侍从讲。

[*Exeunt* AMBASSADORS.

DUKE OF EXETER.

This was a merry message.

KING HENRY.

We hope to make the sender blush at it.
Therefore, my lords, omit no happy hour
That may give furtherance to our expedition;
For we have now no thought in us but France,
Save those to God, that run before our business.
Therefore let our proportions for these wars
Be soon collected, and all things thought upon
That may with reasonable swiftness add
More feathers to our wings; for, God before,
We 'll chide this Dauphin at his father's door.
Therefore let every man now task his thought,
That this fair action may on foot be brought.

[*Flourish. Exeunt.*

301 **omit**：neglect；waste. **happy**：propitious.

302 **give furtherance to**：further；advance.

304 **those**：thoughts (prayers).

305 **proportions**：appointed forces.

308 **God before**：with God leading us.

309 **chide**：chastise；take to task.

310 **task**：fully exercise.

311 **That**：so that. **fair**：just. **on foot be brought**：be set afoot.

ACT II PROLOGUE

Enter CHORUS.

CHORUS.

Now all the youth of England are on fire,
And silken dalliance in the wardrobe lies:
Now thrive the armorers, and honor's thought
Reigns solely in the breast of every man:
They sell the pasture now to buy the horse;
Following the mirror of all Christian kings,
With winged heels, as English Mercuries.
For now sits Expectation in the air,
And hides a sword from hilts unto the point
With crowns imperial, crowns, and coronets,
Promised to Harry and his followers.
The French, advised by good intelligence
Of this most dreadful preparation,
Shake in their fear; and with pale policy
Seek to divert the English purposes.
O England! —model to thy inward greatness,
Like little body with a mighty heart,—
What mightst thou do, that honor would thee do,
Were all thy children kind and natural!
But see thy fault! France hath in thee found out
A nest of hollow bosomes, which he fills
With treacherous crowns; and three corrupted men,—
One, Richard earl of Cambridge; and the second,
Henry Lord Scroop of Masham; and the third,
Sir Thomas Grey, knight, of Northumberland,—
Have, for the gilt of France—O guilt indeed! —
Confirm'd conspiracy with fearful France;

II.Prologue 第二幕开场白。

1 on fire：enthusiastic.

2 silken dalliance：effeminate pleasure-seeking，形象地也可解释为 silk clothing for pleasure-seeking. **in the wardrobe lies**：is laid aside.

3 honor's thought：aspiration for honor.

6 the mirror (pattern, model) **of all Christian kings**：指 Henry V.

7 Mercury [ˈməːkjuri]：罗马神话中众神的信使，帽上和鞋跟都有翅膀，能飞快来去。

8 sits：is.

9 from hilts unto the point：从把到尖，hilt 当时常用多数，由于剑把上的横柄两端伸出，似有两个柄。

10 crowns imperial：the crowns of England and France.

11 Promised：likely to fall to the lot of. **Harry**：见第一幕前开场白 5 行。

12 advised：informed. **intelligence**：情报。

14 pale policy：intrigue，见下 20 行起。

16 model：mould, something that envelops closely.

18 mightst：might 单数第二人称代词 thou 的动词加(e)st 的字尾变化。 **that honor would thee do**：that would be honorable for you to do.

19 Were all thy children：If all your children were. **kind and natural**：loving and devoted as kinsmen (这里是 children) should.

20 fault：flaw.

21 hollow bosoms：false hearts. **he**：France.

22 treacherous crowns：gold coins paid for treachery.

23 Richard earl of Cambridge：cousin of Henry IV.

26 gilt：gold. **guilt**：crime.这两字为同音，双关语。

27 Confirm'd：joined in. **fearful**：full of fear, frightened.

And by their hands this grace of kings must die,
If hell and treason hold their promises,
Ere he take ship for France, and in Southampton.
Linger your patience on; and we 'll digest
Th' abuse of distance; force a play.
The sum is paid; the traitors are agreed;
The king is set from London; and the scene
Is now transported, gentles, to Southampton,—
There is the playhouse now, there must you sit:
And thence to France shall we convey you safe,
And bring you back, charming the narrow seas
To give you gentle pass; for, if we may,
We 'll not offend one stomach with our play.
But, till the king come forth, and not till then,
Unto Southampton do we shift our scene. [*Exit*.

SCENE I

London. Befor the Boar's Head Tavern, Eastcheap.

Enter CORPORAL NYM *and* LIEUTENANT BARDOLPH.

BARDOLPH.

Well met, Corporal Nym.

NYM.

Good morrow, Lieutenant Bardolph.

BARDOLPH.

What, are Ancient Pistol and you friends yet?

NYM.

For my part, I care not: I say little; but when time shall serve, there shall be smiles; — but that shall be as it may. I dare not fight; but I will wink, and hold out mine iron: it is a simple one; but what though? it will toast cheese, and it will endure cold as another man's sword will: and there 's the humor of it.

28 this grace of kings：this king who does honor to the title, meaning Henry V. **must**：和下面的 hold，take 都是假设语气动词。

29 hell and treason：hellish (diabolic) treason. **hold their promises**：succeed.

30 Ere：before. **and in**：while he is at.

31 Linger…on：hold；prolong. **digest**：dispose of.

32 Th' abuse of distance：the difficulty of ignoring distance. **force a play**：produce a play by cramming its events into a short time and small space.

33 sum：price for treason.

34 is set：has set out.

35 gentles：gentlefolk,对观众称呼。

38 charming the narrow seas：casting a spell on the English Channel so that the sea will be calm.

39 pass：passage.

40 offend one stomach：make anybody seasick.

II.i

Corporal：下士。 **Lieutenant**[lef'tenənt]：中尉。

1 Nym：源自德文 nehmen，to take；古英语作 nim 或 nym，to steal.

2 Good morrow：good morning，good day.

3 What：惊叹词。 **are Ancient Pistol and you friends yet?**：Have you made up your quarrel with Ancient Pistol yet? (Mistress Quickly 曾和 Nym 订婚,见下 17 行,但后又嫁给 Pistol,为此两个男人吵了架。) **Ancient**：ensign,旧时掌旗的陆军少尉(最低的受委任军官),相当于 sub-lieutenant,但有时也被称为 Lieutenant (尉官)。

4—5 when time shall serve：when the right time comes.

6 wink：shut my eyes. **hold out**：thrust.

7 iron：sword.

9 humor of it：that is, the ability to adapt to a situation；'humor' is Nym's favorite word.

BARDOLPH.

I will bestow a breakfast to make you friends; and we'll be all three sworn brothers to France: let's be so, good Corporal Nym.

NYM.

Faith, I will live so long as I may, that's the certain of it; and when I cannot live any longer, I will do as I may: that is my rest, that is the rendezvous of it.

BARDOLPH.

It is certain, corporal, that he is married to Nell Quickly: and, certainly, she did you wrong; for you were troth-plight to her.

NYM.

I cannot tell: — things must be as they may: men may sleep, and they may have their throats about them at that time; and, some say, knives have edges. It must be as it may: though patience be a tired mare, yet she will plod. There must be conclusions. Well, I cannot tell.

BARDOLPH.

Here comes Ancient Pistol and his wife: — good corporal, be patient here.

Enter PISTOL *and* HOSTESS.

How now, mine host Pistol!

PISTOL.

Base tike, call'st thou me host?
Now, by this hand, I swear, I scorn the term;
Nor shall my Nell keep lodgers.

HOSTESS.

No, by my troth, not long; for we cannot lodge and board a dozen or fourteen gentlewomen that live honestly by the prick of their needles, but it will be thought we keep a bawdy-house straight. [NYM *and* PISTOL *draw*.] O well-a-day, Lady, if he be not drawn now!

10 **bestow**：provide.

11 **to France**：to go to France.

13 **Faith**：in faith.

13—14 **that's the certain of it**：that's certain.of it 是 Nym 的口头禅之一。

15 **rest**：stake，last throw. **rendezvous** [ˈrɔndivuː，法语]：last resort.

18 **troth-plight**：betrothed.

23 **conclusions**：final settlements.

27 **How now**：How are you now 的省略说法。 **host**：客店老板。

28 **tike**：mongrel，cur. **call'st thou me**：do you call me? 这些地方用 thou 不用 you，有故意侮慢的意思。

30 **Nell**：Mistress Quickly 的名字，系 Helen，Helena 或 Eleanor 的缩称。

31 **by my troth**：in faith. **not long**：not for long.

34 **straight**：immediately.

35 ***draw***：draw out sword，ready to fight. **well-a-day**：alas. **Lady**：by our Lady the Virgin Mary，a mild oath.

We shall see wilful adultery and murder committed.

BARDOLPH.

Good lieutenant, — good corporal, — offer nothing here.

NYM.

Pish!

PISTOL.

Pish for thee, Iceland dog! thou prick-ear'd cur of Iceland!

HOSTESS.

Good Corporal Nym, show thy valor, and put up your sword.

NYM.

Will you shog off? I would have you *solus*.

PISTOL.

Solus, egregious dog? O viper vile!
The *solus* in thy most mervailous face;
The *solus* in thy teeth, and in thy throat,
And in thy hateful lungs, yea, in thy maw, perdy,
And, which is worse, within thy nasty mouth!
I do retort the *solus* in thy bowels;
For I can take, and Pistol's cock is up,
And flashing fire will follow.

NYM.

I am not Barbason; you cannot conjure me. I have an humor to knock you indifferently well. If you grow foul with me, Pistol, I will scour you with my rapier, as I may, in fair terms: if you would walk off, I would prick your guts a little, in good terms, as I may: and that's the humor of it.

PISTOL.

O braggart vile, and damned furious wight!
The grave doth gape, and doting death is near;
Therefore exhale.

BARDOLPH.

36 adultery：The word is used because the two men will be fighting on account of a woman.

37 offer nothing here：There is nothing to fight for here.

39 Iceland dog!：a curl-haired lapdog，used here to show despise. 大概 Nym 的头发很长。

43 shog off：jog off. ***solus***〈拉丁语〉：alone.Pistol 不懂此字，以为是侮辱他。

45 mervailous：marvelous（a sarcasm）.莎士比亚的拼法，重音在第二音节。

47 maw：stomach. **perdy**：par dieu（the French for 'by God'，a mild oath）.

49 retort：return（with a blow）.

50 take：① take offense；② strike. **cock**：手枪扳机。

52 Barbason：the name of a demon.

52—53 I have an humor：I have a mind.

53 indifferently：fairly.

54 foul：① rough；② dirty. **scour**：① punish；②（擦枪杆）clean out.

57 that's the humor of it：that's what I would like to do.

58 wight：fellow.

59 doth gape：opens wide its mouth（ready to receive you）. **doting**：fond.

60 exhale：draw your sword.

Hear me, hear me what I say: — he that strikes the first stroke, I'll run him up to the hilts, as I am a soldier.

[*Draws*.

PISTOL.

An oath of mickle might; and fury shall abate.—
Give me thy fist, thy fore-foot to me give:
Thy spirits are most tall. [*They sheathe their swords*.

NYM.

I will cut thy throat, one time or other, in fair terms: that is the humor of it.

PISTOL.

Couple a gorge!
That is the word. I thee defy again.
O hound of Crete, think'st thou my spouse to get?
No; to the spital go,
And from the powdering-tub of infamy
Fetch forth the lazar kite of Cressid's kind,
Doll Tearsheet she by name, and her espouse:
I have, and I will hold, the *quondam* Quickly
For the only she, and—*pauca*, there's enough.
Go to.

Enter BOY.

BOY.

Mine host Pistol, you must come to my master, — and you, hostess: — he is very sick, and would to bed. — Good Bardolphy, put thy face between his sheets, and do the office of a warming-pan.—Faith, he 's very ill.

BARDOLPH.

Away, you rogue!

HOSTESS.

By my troth, he'll yield the crow a pudding one of these days: the king has kill'd his heart. — Good husband, come home presently.

[*Exeunt* HOSTESS *and* BOY

62 run: make (sword) go into.

63 mickle: much.

64 fist: hand. **fore-foot**: hand.均用 f 开头,押头韵。

65 tall: valiant.

68 *Couple a gorge*!: Pistol's garbled French for "couper la gorge"— cut the throat.

70 hound of Crete:希腊克里特岛产的长毛猎狗。

71 spital: hospital.

72 powdering-tub:腌肉的大木桶,又指蒸气浴木桶,俗信蒸浴可治梅毒。

73 lazar: leper. **kite**: (read 'kit') kitten. **Cressid**: (见莎剧 *Troilus and Cressida*)为中世纪传说中特洛伊妇女,对爱情不忠,后被情夫逐出门外,沦为乞丐并染上麻风病,最终死于医院中。kite, Cressid's 和 kind 三字押头韵。

74 Doll Tearsheet:为一暗娼,见《亨利四世》下篇。

75 quondam: former.

76 she: mistress, love. ***pauca***〈拉丁文〉: pauca verba 即 few words.

77 Boy: Henry V 在做王子时就送给 Falstaff 的侍童。

78 my master: Sir John Falstaff,没落的胖骑士,生活放荡,语言幽默,是 Henry V 年轻时的伙伴。见《亨利四世》上下篇、《温莎的风流娘儿们》。

79 would to bed: is obliged to lie in bed.

81 warming-pan:有长柄的扁圆铜盘,空心的盘内可放炭火,用以烘烤床单取暖。Bardolph 有红色的酒糟鼻,人们取笑他的脸像炭火。

83 yield the crow a pudding: become carrion for the crow; i.e. die.

84 the king has kill'd his heart: Henry V 登基后断绝了同 Falstaff 的关系,见《亨利四世》下篇。

85 presently: at once.

BARDOLPH.

Come, shall I make you two friends? We must to France together: why the devil should we keep knives to cut one another's throats?

PISTOL.

Let floods o'erswell, and fiends for food howl on!

NYM.

You'll pay me the eight shillings I won of you at betting?

PISTOL.

Base is the slave that pays.

NYM.

That now I will have: that's the humor of it.

PISTOL.

As manhood shall compound: push home.

[*They draw*.

BARDOLPH.

By this sword, he that makes the first thrust, I'll kill him; by this sword, I will. [*Draws*.

PISTOL.

Sword is an oath, and oaths must have their course.

BARDOLPH.

Corporal Nym, an thou wilt be friends, be friends: an thou wilt not, why, then be enemies with me too. Prithee, put up.

NYM.

I shall have my eight shillings I won of you at betting?

PISTOL.

A noble shalt thou have, and present pay;
And liquor likewise will I give to thee,
And friendship shall combine and brotherhood;
I'll live by Nym, and Nym shall live by me;—
Is not this just? —for I shall sutler be
Unto the camp, and profits will accrue.
Give me thy hand. [*They sheathe their swords*.]

89 **Let…on!**：Let things take their own course，听其自然。

91 **Base is…pays**：这是一句成语。

92 **That now I will have**：I must have that money now.

93 **As manhood shall compound**：As a brave man will settle such a dispute. **push**：thrust (with a weapon).

94 **By this sword**：I swear by the sword.

96 **Sword**：to swear by a sword.

97 **an**：if.

99 **put up**：sheathe the sword.

100 **I shall have**：am I to have.

101 **noble**：一种硬币，值 6 先令 8 便士。 **present pay**：immediat payment.

104 **Nym**：此字有 taker，thief 的意思。

105 **sutler**：provisioner to the army.

NYM.

I shall have my noble?

PISTOL.

In cash most justly paid.

NYM.

Well, then, that's the humor of it.

Enter HOSTESS.

HOSTESS.

As ever you came of women, come in quickly to Sir John. Ah, poor heart! he is so shaked of a burning quotidian tertian, that it is most lamentable to behold. Sweet men, come to him.

NYM.

The king hath run bad humors on the knight, that's the even of it.

PISTOL.

Nym, thou hast spoke the right;
His heart is fracted and corroborate.

NYM.

The king is a good king: but it must be as it may; he passes some humors and careers.

PISTOL.

Let us condole the knight; for, lambkings, we will live.

[*Exeunt*.

SCENE II

Southampton. A council-chamber.

Enter EXETER, BEDFORD, *and* WESTMORELAND.

DUKE OF BEDFORD.

'Fore God, his Grace is bold, to trust these traitors.

DUKE OF EXETER.

They shall be apprehended by and by.

EARL OF WESTMORELAND.

111 came of: issued from, were born by.

112 shaked of: shaken by.

113 quotidian tertian: she is mixed up on her medical terms; a quotidian is a fever recurring every day, a tertian every three days.

114 Sweet: dear.

115 run bad humors on the knight: lost his temper with the knight; been displeased with the knight. **run bad humors on**: upset by his displeasure.

116 even: plain truth.

118 fracted and corroborate: Pistol's term for 'broken',实际上 corroborate 意为 strengthened.

120 passes some humors and careers: indulge in some whims and pranks (to pass the career in horsemanship means to do a short gallop at full stretch).

121 condole: show sympathy with. **lambkins**: little lambs (a term of endearment).

II.ii

Bedford: Duke of Bedford，即 John of Lancaster，是 Henry V 亲二弟。

1 'Fore God: before God (a mild oath).

2 apprehended: arrested.

How smooth and even they do bear themselves!
As if allegiance in their bosoms sat,
Crowned with faith and constant loyalty.

DUKE OF BEDFORD.

The king hath note of all that they intend,
By interception which they dream not of.

DUKE OF EXETER.

Nay, but the man that was his bedfellow,
Whom he hath dull'd and cloy'd with gracious favors,
That he should, for a foreign purse, so sell
His sovereign's life to death and treachery!

Trumpets sound. Enter KING HENRY, CAMBRIDGE, SCROOP, GREY, LORDS, *and* ATTENDANTS.

KING HENRY.

Now sits the wind fair, and we will aboard.
My Lord of Cambridge, — and my kind Lord of Masham,
And you, my gentle knight, — give me your thoughts:
Think you not that the powers we bear with us
Will cut their passage through the force of France,
Doing the execution and the act
For which we have in head assembled them?

LORD SCROOP.

No doubt, my liege, if each man do his best.

KING HENRY.

I doubt not that; since we are well persuaded
We carry not a heart with us from hence
That grows not in a fair consent with ours,
Nor leave not one behind that doth not wish
Success and conquest to attend on us.

EARL OF CAMBRIDGE.

Never was monarch better fear'd and loved
Than is your majesty: there's not, I think, a subject
That sits in heart-grief and uneasiness

3 **smooth and even**: bland and calm.

6 **hath note of**: has taken note of; has been informed of.

7 **By interception**: by intercepting their correspondence with the enemy.

8 **bedfellow**: Henry Scroop of Masham, 曾是 Henry V 的好友。

9 **dull'd**: bored; tired. **cloy'd**: glutted; satiated.

10 **purse**: bribe.

12 **sits**: 风比较稳定地来自一个方向。

15 **powers**: troops.

16 **cut their passage through**: fight their way through.

17 **Doing the execution and the act**: fulfiling the task.

18 **in head**: as an armed force. **them**: 指上文 powers.

20 **persuaded**: convinced, 下面省略 that.

22 **grows not**: does not quicken the tempo of its beat. **consent**: agreement. **ours**: my heart.

23 **Nor leave not**: 用两个否定词,为强调的否定,当时常用。

25 **better fear'd**: more revered.

27 **sits**: lives. **heart-grief**: sorrow.

Under the sweet shade of your government.

SIR THOMAS GREY.

True: those that were your father's enemies
Have steept their galls in honey, and do serve you
With hearts create of duty and of zeal.

KING HENRY.

We therefore have great cause of thankfulness;
And shall forget the office of our hand,
Sooner than quittance of desert and merit
According to the weight and worthiness.

LORD SCROOP.

So service shall with steeled sinews toil,
And labour shall refresh itself with hope,
To do your Grace incessant services.

KING HENRY.

We judge no less.—Uncle of Exeter,
Enlarge the man committed yesterday,
That rail'd against our person: we consider
It was excess of wine that set him on;
And, on his more advice, we pardon him.

LORD SCROOP.

That's mercy, but too much security:
Let him be punisht, sovereign; lest example
Breed, by his sufferance, more of such a kind.

KING HENRY.

O, let us yet be merciful.

EARL OF CAMBRIDGE.

So may your highness, and yet punish too.

SIR THOMAS GREY.

Sir, you show great mercy, if you give him life,
After the taste of much correction.

KING HENRY.

Alas, your too much love and care of me
Are heavy orisons 'gainst this poor wretch!

30 **steept**: soaked. **galls**: bitterness.

31 **create**: created; made.中世纪英语中,以 t 音结尾的动词,其完成体常不再加-ed.

33 **office**: use.参看《圣经·旧约·诗篇》第 137 章 5 节:"If I forget thee, O Jerusalem, let my right hand forget her cunning."

34 **Sooner than**: sooner than to forget. **quittance**: due reward. **desert** [diˈzəːt]: merit.

35 **weight**: importance.

36 **steeled sinews**: strengthened vigor.

40 **Enlarge**: set free. **committed**: committed to prison.

41 **rail'd against**: spoke out against.

43 **on his more advice**: on his thinking better of it.

44 **security**: confidence.

46 **Breed**: bring forward. **sufferance**: being allowed to go unpunished.

49 **give him life**: spare his life.

50 **correction**: punishment.

52 **heavy orisons**: weighty pleas.

If little faults, proceeding on distemper,
Shall not be winkt at, how shall we stretch our eye
When capital crimes, chew'd, swallow'd, and digested,
Appear before us? —We 'll yet enlarge that man,
Though Cambridge, Scroop, and Grey, in their dear care
And tender preservation of our person,
Would have him punisht. And now to our French causes:
Who are the late commissioners?

EARL OF CAMBRIDGE.

I one, my lord:
Your highness bade me ask for it to-day.

LORD SCROOP.

So did you me, my liege.

SIR THOMAS GREY.

And me, my royal sovereign.

KING HENRY.

Then, Richard earl of Cambridge, there is yours;—
There yours, Lord Scroop of Masham;—and, sir knight,
Grey of Northumberland, this same is yours:—
Read them; and know, I know your worthiness.—
My Lord of Westmoreland, and uncle Exeter,
We will aboard to-night.—Why, how now, gentlemen!
What see you in those papers, that you lose
So much complexion? —Look ye, how they change!
Their cheeks are paper.—Why, what read you there,
That hath so cowarded and chased your blood
Out of appearance?

EARL OF CAMBRIDGE.

I do confess my fault;
And do submit me to your highness' mercy.

SIR THOMAS GREY *and* LORD SCROOP.

To which we all appeal.

KING HENRY.

The mercy that was quick in us but late,

53 **proceeding on**: arising from. **distemper**: intemperance; drunkenness.

54 **winkt** (winked) **at**: overlooked. **stretch**: open wide.

55 **chew'd, swallow'd, and digested**: committed after premeditation.

59 **now to**: now let's turn our attention to.

60 **late**: lately appointed. **commissioners**: persons appointed to act for the king during his absence in France.

61 **I one**: I am one of them.

62 **it**: commission.

65 **yours**: your commission, a piece of paper the King hands to him.

68 **worthiness**: here used in an ironical sense.

71—72 **lose…complexion**: turn pale.

72 **Look ye**: note. (This remark is addressed to the lords in attendence other than the three traitors.)

73 **paper**: as white as paper.

74 **so cowarded**: make such cowards of, so terrified.

75 **appearance**: countenance.

77 **which**: your highness' mercy.

78 **quick**: alive. **but**: only. **late**: recently.

By your own counsel is supprest and kill'd:
You must not dare, for shame, to talk of mercy;
For your own reasons turn into your bosoms,
As dogs upon their masters, worrying you.—
See you, my princes and my noble peers,
These English monsters! My Lord of Cambridge here,—
You know how apt our love was to accord
To furnish him with all appertinents
Belonging to his honor; and this man
Hath, for a few light crowns, lightly conspired,
And sworn unto the practices of France,
To kill us here in Hampton: to the which
This knight, no less for bounty bound to us
Than Cambridge is, hath likewise sworn. —But, O,
What shall I say to thee, Lord Scroop? thou cruel,
Ingrateful, savage, and inhuman creature!
Thou that didst bear the key of all my counsels,
That knew'st the very bottom of my soul,
That almost mightst have coin'd me into gold,
Wouldst thou have practised on me for thy use,—
May it be possible, that foreign hire
Could out of thee extract one spark of evil
That might annoy my finger? 'tis so strange,
That, though the truth of it stands off as gross
As black from white, my eye will scarcely see it.
Treason and murder ever kept together,
As two yoke-devils sworn to either's purpose,
Working so grossly in a natural cause,
That admiration did not whoop at them:
But thou, 'gainst all proportion, didst bring in
Wonder to wait on treason and on murder:
And whatsoever cunning fiend it was
That wrought upon thee so preposterously,

81 **reasons**: arguments. **turn into your bosoms**: turn on yourselves.

82 **worrying**: savaging.

85 **apt**: read; willing. **accord**: agree.

86 **appertinents**: appurtenances.

87 **Belonging to**: suiting.

88 **for a few light crowns**: for a petty sum. **lightly**: readily.

89 **practices**: plots.

90 **Hampton**: southampton. **the which**: the practices of France.

91 **bounty**: generosity. **bound**: obliged.

94 **Ingrateful**: ungrateful.

95 **bear the key of all my counsels**: have access to all my secret thoughts.

97—98 **mightst have… for thy use**: you might have turned me into gold coins for your use. **practiced on**: used some strategem on.

101 **amnoy**: harm; hurt.

102 **stands off**: stands out. **gross**: palpable; evident.

104 **ever**: always.

106 **grossly**: obviously; glaringly.

107 **admiration**: wonder; surprise. **whoop**: cry out.

108 **proportion**: natural order.

109 **Wonder**: astonishment. **wait on**: accompany.

111 **preposterously**: perversely.

Hath got the voice in hell for excellence:
And other devils, that suggest by treasons,
Do botch and bungle up damnation
With patches, colors, and with forms being fetcht
From glistering semblances of piety;
But he that temper'd thee bade thee stand up,
Gave thee no instance why thou shouldst do treason,
Unless to dub thee with the name of traitor.
If that same demon that hath gull'd thee thus
should with his lion-gait walk the whole world,
He might return to vasty Tartar back,
And tell the legions, 'I can never win
A soul so easy as that Englishman's.'
O,how hast thou with jealousy infected
The sweetness of affiance! Show men dutiful?
Why, so didst thou: seem they grave and learned?
Why, so didst thou: come they of noble family?
Why, so didst thou: seem they religious?
Why, so didst thou: or are they spare in diet;
Free from gross passion, or of mirth or anger;
Constant in spirit, not swerving with the blood;
Garnisht and deckt in modest complement;
Not working with the eye without the ear,
And but in purged judgement trusting neither?
Such and so finely bolted didst thou seem:
And thus thy fall hath left a kind of blot,
To mark the full-fraught man and best indued
With some suspicion. I will weep for thee;
For this revolt of thine, methinks,is like
Another fall of man.—Their faults are open:
Arrest them to the answer of the law;—
And God acquit them of their practices!

DUKE OF EXETER.

I arrest thee of high treason, by the name of Richard

112 **voice**: vote.

113 **suggest**: temp; lead astray.

114 **botch and bungle up**: repair and disguise in a clumsy way. **damnation**: damnable deeds.

117 **temper'd**: worked upon.

118 **instance**: reason; motive.

120 **gull'd**: deceived.

121 **lion-gait**: devil's stride,参看《圣经·新约·彼得前书》第5章8节:"… your adversary the devil, as a roaring lion, walketh about, seeking whom he may devour."

122 **vasty**: wide and waste. **Tartar**: Tartarus,希腊、罗马神话中的地狱。

123 **legions**: host of devils.

125 **jealousy**: suspicion. **infect**: contaminate.

126 **affiance**: confidence. **Show men dutiful?**: Do men appear to be dutiful?

132 **the blood**: passion.

133 **Garnisht and deckt** (garnished and decked): wellsupplied and embellished. **complement**: qualities that go to "complete" the character of a gentleman.

134 Not trusting their eyes without seeking confirmation by inquiry.

135 **purged**: sober. **neither**: neither the eye nor the ear.

136 **finely bolted**: sifted like the finest flour; refined.

137 **fall**: 堕落,参看141行,fall of man(人类的堕落),指亚当的堕落,见《圣经·旧约·创世记》第3章。

138 **full-fraught**: gifted. **indued**: endowed.

141 **faults**: crimes; offences. **open**: evident.

142 **to the answer of**: in accordance with.

143 **practices**: plots.

144 第一个 **of**: for,下同。

earl of Cambridge.
I arrest thee of high treason, by the name of Henry
Lord Scroop of Masham.
I arrest thee of high treason, by the name of Thomas
Grey, knight, of Northumberland.

LORD SCROOP.

Our purposes God justly hath discover'd;
And I repent my fault more than my death;
Which I beseech your highness to forgive,
Although my body pay the price of it.

EARL OF CAMBRIDGE.

For me,—the gold of France did not seduce;
Although I did admit it as a motive
The sooner to effect what I intended:
But God be thanked for prevention;
Which I in sufferance heartily will rejoice,
Beseeching God and you to pardon me.

SIR THOMAS GREY.

Never did faithful subject more rejoice
At the discovery of most dangerous treason
Than I do at this hour joy o'er myself,
Prevented from a damned enterprise:
My fault, but not my body, pardon, sovereign.

KING HENRY.

God quit you in his mercy! Hear your sentence.
You have conspired against our royal person,
Join'd with an enemy proclaim'd, and from his coffers
Received the golden earnest of our death;
Wherein you would have sold your king to slaughter,
His princes and his peers to servitude,
His subjects to oppression and contempt,
And his whole kingdom into desolation.
Touching our person, seek we no revenge;
But we our kingdom's safety must so tender,

150 **discover'd**: revealed; uncovered.

155 **admit**: accept.

156 **what I intended**: to secure the throne for his wife's brother Edmund Mortimer, the Earl of March, who was expected to die and be succeeded by Cambridge's heirs as next in line.

158 **sufferance**: suffering, the penalty of death.

162 **joy o'er myself**: rejoice in my own misfortune.

165 **quit**: acquit; absolve.

168 **earnest**: part-payment in advance as a pledge of a bargain.

169 **Wherein**: 后省略条件从句 if you had succeeded.

173 **Touching our person**: regarding myself personally.

174 **tender**: tend; watch over.

Whose ruin you have sought, that to her laws
We do deliver you. Get you, therefore, hence,
Poor miserable wretches, to your death:
The taste whereof, God of his mercy give
You patience to endure, and true repentance
Of all your dear offences! —Bear them hence.
[*Exeunt* CAMBRIDGE, SCROOP, *and* GREY, *guarded*.
Now, lords, for France; the enterprise whereof
Shall be to you as us like glorious.
We doubt not of a fair and lucky war,
Since God so graciously hath brought to light
This dangerous treason, lurking in our way
To hinder our beginnings; we doubt not now
But every rub is smoothed on our way.
Then, forth, dear countrymen: let us deliver
Our puissance into the hand of God,
Putting it straight in expedition.
Cheerly to sea; the signs of war advance:
No king of England, if not king of France. [*Exeunt*.

SCENE III

London. Before the Boar's-Head Tavern, Eastcheap.

Enter PISTOL, HOSTESS, NYM, BARDOLPH, *and* BOY.

HOSTESS.

Prithee, honey-sweet husband, let me bring thee to Staines.

PISTOL.

No; for my manly heart doth yearn.—
Bardolph, be blithe; — Nym, rouse thy vaunting veins; —
Boy, bristle thy courage up; — for Falstaff he is dead,
And we must yearn therefore.

BARDOLPH.

175 **that**: coordinate with the adverb 'so' in the above line.

178 **whereof**: of which (your death). **of his mercy**: out of mercy.

180 **dear**: dire. **Bear**: carry; take.

182 **like**: alike.

187 **rub**: hindrance;地滚球戏中地面上不平的障碍物叫 rub.

189 **puissance**: armed force.

190 **straight**: immediately. **expedition**: speedy motion.

191 **Cheerly**: cheerfully. **to sea**: 英舰只于 1415 年 8 月 11 日从 Southampton 启航。 **signs**: banners; standards. **advance**: raise; lift up.

II.iii

1 **Prithee**: pray you, please. **bring**: escort.

2 **Staines**: Staines Bridge over the Thames, the first stage stop on the road to southampton.

3 **yearn**: grieve.

4 **be blithe**: cheer up. **rouse thy vaunting veins**: call forth your usual boastful spirits.

5 **bristle…up**: pluck up. **he**: an expletive used here for emphasis.

Would I were with him, wheresome'er he is, either in heaven or in hell!

HOSTESS.

Nay, sure, he's not in hell: he's in Arthur's bosom, if ever man went to Arthur's bosom. A' made a finer end, and went away, an it had been any christom child; a' parted ev'n just between twelve and one, ev'n at the turning o' th' tide: for after I saw him fumble with the sheets, and play with flowers, and smile upon his fingers' ends, I knew there was but one way; for his nose was as sharp as a pen, and a' babbled of green fields. 'How now, Sir John!' quoth I: 'what, man! be o' good cheer.' So a' cried out 'God, God, God!' three or four times. Now I, to comfort him, bid him a' should not hink of God; I hoped there was no need to trouble himself with any such thoughts yet. So a' bade me lay more clothes on his feet: I put my hand into the bed and felt them, and they were as cold as any stone; then I felt to his knees, and they were as cold as any stone; and so upward and upward, and all was as cold as any stone.

NYM.

They say he cried out of sack.

HOSTESS.

Ay, that a' did.

BARDOLPH.

And of women.

HOSTESS.

Nay, that a' did not.

BOY.

Yes, that a' did; and said they were devils incarnate.

HOSTESS.

A' could never abide carnation; 'twas a color he never liked.

BOY.

7 **Would**: I wish. **wheresome'er**: wherever.

9 **Arthur's bosom**: Mistress Quickly probably mixes King Arthur with Abraham,参看《圣经·新约·路加福音》第16章22节"... the beggar died, and was carried by the angels into Abraham's bosom," i.e., heaven.

10 **A'**: he. **a finer end**: i.e., than many a one I've seen.

11 **an it**: as if he. **christom child**: newly christened child.

12 **parted**: departed. **ev'n**: even.

12—13 **at the turning o'th'tide**: It was then a popular belief that a dying person will live till the tide turns.

15 **but one way**: i.e. only death.

17 **quoth**: said.

22 **them**: his feet.

26 **of**: against,26行同。 **sack**: 白葡萄酒。

30 **incarnate**: ① embodied in flesh; ② flesh-colored or crimson, hence the following remark by Mistress Quickly.

31 **abide**: endure; tolerate. **carnation**: the color of flesh, rosy pink.

A' said once, the devil would have him about women.

HOSTESS.

A' did in some sort, indeed, handle women; but then he was rheumatic, and talkt of the whore of Babylon.

BOY.

Do you not remember, a'saw a flea stick upon Bardolph's nose, and a' said it was a black soul burning in hell-fire?

BARDOLPH.

Well, the fuel is gone that maintain'd that fire: that's all the riches I got in his service.

NYM.

Shall we shog? the king will be gone from Southampton.

PISTOL.

Come, let's away. —My love, give me thy lips.
Look to my chattels and my movables:
Let senses rule; the word is 'Pitch and pay;'
Trust none;
For oaths are straws, men's faiths are wafer-cakes,
And hold-fast is the only dog, my duck:
Therefore, *caveto* be thy counsellor.
Go, clear thy crystals. —Yoke-fellows in arms,
Let us to France; like horse-leeches, my boys,
To suck, to suck, the very blood to suck!

BOY.

And that's but unwholesome food, they say.

PISTOL.

Touch her soft mouth, and march.

BARDOLPH.

Farewell, hostess. [*Kissing her*.

NYM.

I cannot kiss, that is the humor of it; but; adieu.

PISTOL.

Let housewifery appear: keep close, I thee command.

HOSTESS.

33 **about women**：because of his weakness for women.

35 **rheumatic**：错用来指 delirious. **whore of Babylon**：见《圣经·旧约·启示录》第 17 章 3—5 节，巴比伦的淫妇之母。

37 **black soul**：lost soul.

38 **fuel**：指酒。

39 **riches**：参酒，a rich nose＝a red nose.

40 **shog**：be off.

41 **let's away**：let us go away，这类行动动词常可省略。

43 **Let senses rule**：Keep your wits about you. **'Pitch and pay'**：（成语）pay on the spot；no credit.

45 **strawa**：trifles. **wafer-cakes**：brittle and thin cakes.

46 **hold-fast is the only dog**：（成语）"Brag is a good dog，but hold-fast is a better." **duck**：darling；dear.

47 **caveto**〈拉丁语〉：cave＝beware.

48 **crystals**：eyes. **Yoke-fellows**：companions.

55 **Let housewifery appear**：let good management（thrift）take over. **keep close**：stay at home.

Farewell; adieu. [*Exeunt.*

SCENE IV

France. A room in the French KING'S *palace.*

Flourish. Enter the French KING, *the* DAUPHIN, *the* DUKE OF BURGUNDY, *the* CONSTABLE, *and others.*

FRENCH KING.

Thus comes the English with full power upon us;
And more than carefully it us concerns
To answer royally in our defenses.
Therefore the Dukes of Berri and of Bretagne,
Of Brabant and of Orleans, shall make forth,—
And you, Prince Dauphin,—with all swift dispatch,
To line and new repair our towns of war
With men of courage and with means defendant;
For England his approaches makes as fierce
As waters to the sucking of a gulf.
It fits us, then, to be as provident
As fear may teach us, out of late examples
Left by the fatal and neglected English
Upon our fields.

DAUPHIN.

My most redoubted father,
It is most meet we arm us 'gainst the foe;
For peace itself should not so dull a kingdom,
Though war nor no known quarrel were in question,
But that defenses, musters, preparations,
Should be maintain'd, assembled, and collected,
As were a war in expectation.
Therefore, I say 'tis meet we all go forth
To view the sick and feeble parts of France:
And let us do it with no show of fear;
No, with no more than if we heard that England

II.iv

Flourish：响亮的喇叭乐声，在国王上场或起立准备下场时吹奏。

2 carefully：with care and anxiety.

5 Orleans：Louis Duke of Orléans，是 Charles VI 的弟弟。**make forth**：set out.

6 dispatch：speed；expedition.

7 line：strengthen. **new**：anew.

8 defendant：of defense.

9 England：the King of England. **his approaches makes**：makes his approaches. **fierce**：violently.

10 gulf：whirlpool.

11 fits：befits. **provident**：cautious.

12 out of：(referring to 'fear') caused by. **late examples**：the English victories at Crécy (1346) and Poitiesr.

13 fatal and neglected：deadly and underestimated.

14 redoubted：dreaded；revered.

15 meet：fitting. **us**：ourselves. **'gainst**：against.

16 dull：make dull；benumb.

17 Though war：though no war. **in question**：at issue.

18 But that：but. **musters**：recruitments.

20 As were a war：as if a war were.

22 view：inspect. **sick and feeble**：badly and inadequately fortified.

Were busied with a Whitsun morris-dance:
For, my good liege, she is so idly king'd,
Her scepter so fantastcally borne
By a vain, giddy, shallow, humorous youth,
That fear attends her not.

CONSTABLE OF FRANCE.

O peace, Prince Dauphin!
You are too much mistaken in this king:
Question your Grace the late ambassadors,—
With what great state he heard their embassy,
How well supplied with noble counsellors,
How modest in exception, and withal
How terrible in constant resolution,—
And you shall find his vanities forespent
Were but the outside of the Roman Brutus,
Covering discretion with a coat of folly;
As gardeners do with ordure hide those roots
That shall first spring and be most delicate.

DAUPHIN.

Well, 'tis not so, my lord high-constable;
But though we think it so, it is no matter:
In cases of defense 'tis best to weigh
The enemy more mighty than he seems:
So the proportions of defense are fill'd;
Which, of a weak and niggardly projection,
Doth, like a miser, spoil his coat with scanting
A little cloth.

FRENCH KING.

Think we King Harry strong;
And princes, look you strongly arm to meet him.
The kindred of him hath been flesht upon us;
And he is bred out of that bloody strain
That haunted us in our familiar paths:
Witness our too-much memorable shame

25 **Whitsun**：白色星期日，也叫降灵节，为复活节后的第七个星期日，一般在五月底、六月初。 **morris-dance**：15世纪以来英格兰一种民间舞，系从西班牙传来的一种摩尔人舞蹈，故叫摩里斯舞。

26 **she**：England. **so idly king'd**：ruled by such an empty-headed king.

27 **fantastically**：strangely；whimsically.

28 **humorous**：capricious.

29 that she (England) is not to be feared. **peace**：say no more.

31 **Question**：ask. **the late ambassadors**：the ambassadors just back from England.

32 **state**：dignity.

34 **modest in exception**：moderate in raising objections. **withal**：also；besides.

35 **constant**：unshaken.

36 **forespent**：formerly indulged.

37 **outside**：appearance. **the Roman Brutus**：Lucius Junius Brutus of the 6th c. B.C.，who feigned stupidity in order to free Rome from the tyrannous Tarquins.

39 **ordure**：manure.

40 **spring**：put forth shoots.

43 **weigh**：estimate.

45 **proportions**：forces and supplies required for war. **fill'd**：fully provided.

46 **Which**：if planned too scantily.

47 **scanting**：saving.

49 **look you strongly arm**：take care to arm yourselves strongly.

50 **kindred of him**：Henry V's ancestors（曾祖）Edward III 和大伯祖 Edward the Black Prince. **hath been flesht upon us**：尝过我们的血肉。用生肉喂猎狗，使之勇于咬兽叫 to flesh.

51 **strain**：race

52 **haunted**：pursued. **familiar path**：homeland.

When Cressy battle fatally was struck,
And all our princes captived by the hand
Of that black name, Edward, Black Prince of Wales;
Whiles that his mountain sire,—on mountain standing,
Up in the air, crown'd with the golden sun,—
Saw his heroical seed, and smiled to see him,
Mangle the work of nature, and deface
The patterns that by God and by French fathers
Had twenty years been made. This is a stem
Of that victorious stock; and let us fear
The native mightiness and fate of him.

Enter a MESSENGER.

MESSENGER.

Ambassadors from Harry king of England
Do crave admittance to your majesty.

FRENCH KING.

We'll give them present audience. Go, and bring them.

[*Exeunt* MESSENGER *and certain* LORDS.

You see this chase is hotly follow'd, friends.

DAUPHIN.

Turn head, and stop pursuit; for coward dogs
Most spend their mouths, when what they seem to threaten
Runs far before them. Good my sovereign,
Take up the English short; and let them know
Of what a monarchy you are the head:
Self-love, my liege, is not so vile a sin
As self-neglecting.

Enter LORDS, *with* EXETER *and* TRAIN.

FRENCH KING.

From our brother England?

DUKE OF EXETER.

From him; and thus he greets your majesty.
He wills you, in the name of God Almighty,

54 **Cressy**: Crécy.

57 **Whiles that**: while. **his mountain sire**: Edward III, who was born in the mountains of Wales.

59 **seed**: son; offspring.

60 **deface**: destroy.

61 **patterns**: patterned fields and vineyards.

62 **stem**: offspring.

64 **fate**: what he is destined to achieve.

67 **present**: immediate.

68 **hotly**: closely.

69 **Turn head**: turn around; 打猎用语，相当于 stand at bay. **coward**: cowardly.

70 **Most spend their mouths**: bark the most.

71 **Good my sovereign**: my good sovereign.

72 **Take up…short**: interrupt, retort in a short manner.

75 **TRAIN**: retinue.

77 **wills**: bids.

That you divest yourself, and lay apart
The borrow'd glories, that, by gift of heaven,
By law of nature and of nations, 'longs
To him and to his heirs; namely, the crown,
And all wide-stretchèd honors that pertain,
By custom and the ordinance of times,
Unto the crown of France. That you may know
'Tis no sinister nor no awkeward claim,
Pickt from the worm-holes of long-vanisht days,
Nor from the dust of old oblivion raked,
He sends you this most memorable line,
[*Gives a paper*.
In every branch truly demonstrative;
Willing you overlook this pedigree:
And when you find him evenly derived
From his most famed of famous ancestors,
Edward the Third, he bids you then resign
Your crown and kingdom, indirectly held
From him the native and true challenger.

FRENCH KING.

Or else what follows?

DUKE OF EXETER.

Bloody constraint; for if you hide the crown
Even in your hearts, there will he rake for it:
Therefore in fierce tempest is he coming,
In thunder and in earthquanke, like a Jove,
That, if requiring fail, he will compel;
And bids you, in the bowels of the Lord,
Deliver up the crown; and to take mercy
On the poor souls for whom this hungry war
Opens his vasty jaws: and on your head
Turning the widows' tears, the orphans' cries,
The dead men's blood, the pining maidens' groans,
For husbands, fathers, and betrothed lovers,

80 **'longs**：belongs.

82 **wide-stretchèd**：wide-ranging.

83 **ordinance of times**：time-honored usage.

84 **That**：和 78 行的 That 同位。

85 **sinister**：illegimate. **awkward**：perverse.

86 **worm-holes**：worm-eaten documents.

87 Nor raked from…

88 **memorable**：easily remembered；serving to remind. **line**：pedigree；family chart.

89 **demonstrative**：giving evidence or conclusive proof.

90 **Willing**：desiring. **overlook**：look over；read.

91 **evenly**：directly；in a straight line. **derived**：descended.

94 **indirectly**：by crooked method；unfairly.

95 **challenger**：claimant.

97 **Bloody constraint**：war.

99 **fierce**〔读作两音节〕：violent.

100 **Jove**：Jupiter，罗马神话中众神之王，以雷为武器。

101 **requiring**：demanding；asking.

102 **in the bowels of the Lord**：by God's mercy. 参看《圣经·新约·腓立比书》第 1 章 8 节"基督耶稣的心肠"。

103 **take mercy**：have mercy.

105 **vasty**：vast；huge.

105—106 **on your head/Turning**：responsibility (for the following) falling on you.

That shall be swallow'd in this controversy.
This is his claim, his threatening, and my message;
Unless the Dauphin be in presence here,
To whom expressly I bring greeting too.

FRENCH KING.

For us, we will consider of this further:
To-morrow shall you bear our full intent
Back to our brother England.

DAUPHIN.

For the Dauphin,
I stand here for him: what to him from England?

DUKE OF EXETER.

Scorn and defiance; slight regard, contempt,
And any thing that may not misbecome
The mighty sender, doth he prize you at.
Thus says my king: an if your father's highness
Do not, in grant of all demands at large,
Sweeten the bitter mock you sent his majesty,
He'll call you to so hot an answer of it,
That caves and womby vaultages of France
Shall chide your trespass, and return your mock
In second accent of his ordnance.

DAUPHIN.

Say, if my father render fair rerurn,
It is against my will; for I desire
Nothing but odds with England: to that end,
As matching to his youth and vanity,
I did present him with the Paris balls.

DUKE OF EXETER.

He'll make your Paris Louvre shake for it,
Were it the mistress-court of mighty Europe:
And, be assured, you'll find a difference,
As we, his subjects, have in wonder found,
Between the promise of his greener days

111 **Unless**: if.
112 **expressly**: under express order.
117 **regard**: estimation.
118 **misbecome**: misfit; be unworthy of.
119 **prize**: estimate.
120 **an if**: if.
121 **in grant of**: by assenting to. **at large**: in full.
124 **womby**: hollw. **vaultages**: cannon.
126 **second accent**: echo. **ordnance**: caverns.
129 **odds**: quarrel; strife.
130 **matching**: suitable. **vanity**: silliness; frivolity.
131 **Paris balls**: tennis balls.
132 **Louvre**: 卢浮宫,读音与'lover'相似。
133 **Were it**: even if it were. **mistress**: chief; first.
136 **greener**: younger.

And these he masters now: now he weighs time,
Even to the utmost grain: —that you shall read
In your own losses, if he stay in France.

FRENCH KING.

To-morrow shall you know our mind at full.

DUKE OF EXETER.

Dispatch us with all speed, lest that our king
Come here himself to question our delay;
For he is footed in this land already.

FRENCH KING.

You shall be soon dispatcht with fair conditions.
A night is but small breath and little pause
To answer matters of this consequence.

[*Flourish. Exeunt.*

137 **these**: the qualities. **masters**: possesses. **weighs**: puts great value upon.

138 **grain**: tiny quantity. **read**: learn.

139 **In**: to.

143 **is footed**: has landed.

144 **dispatcht**: sent back.

145 **breath**: breathing-space.

146 **this consequence**: such importance.

ACT III PROLOGUE

Enter CHORUS.

CHORUS.
Thus with imagined wing our swift scene flies,
In motion of no less celerity
Than that of thought. Suppose that you have seen
The well-appointed king at Hampton pier
Embark his royalty; and his brave fleet
With silken streamers the young Phœbus fanning:
Play with your fancies; and in them behold
Upon the hempen tackle ship-boys climbing;
Hear the shrill whistle which doth order give
To sounds confused; behold the threaden sails,
Borne with th' invisible and creeping wind,
Draw the huge bottoms through the furrow'd sea,
Breasting the lofty surge: O, do but think
You stand upon the rivage and behold
A city on th' inconstant billows dancing;
For so appears this fleet majestical,
Holding due course to Harfleur. Follow, follow!
Grapple your minds to sternage of this navy;
And leave your England, as dead midnight still,
Guarded with grandsires, babies, and old women,
Either past, or not arrived to, pith and puissance;
For who is he, whose chin is but enricht
With one appearing hair, that will not follow
These cull'd and choice-drawn cavaliers to France?
Work, work your thoughts, and therein see a siege;
Behold the ordnance on their carriages,
With fatal mouths gaping on girded Harfleur.

III.Prologue 第三幕开场白。

1 with imagined wing：on the wings of imagination.

2 celerity：swiftness.

4 well-appointed：well-equipped. **Hampton**：Southampton，英国南部海港骚散普顿(一译南安普顿)。

5 royalty：the ship with the emblem of his royalty. **brave**：splendid.

6 silken streamers：silk banners. **young Phœbus**：the morning sun.Phœbus[ˈfiːbəs]，希腊神话中之日神。本行的自然次序为 with silken streamers fanning the young Phæbus.

9—10 正常字序为 doth give order/To confused sounds.

10 threaden：i.e.，woven of thread.

11 Borne with：driven by.

12 bottoms：keels；ships.

13 Breasting：moving forward against. **lofty surge**：high waves.

14 rivage：shore.

15 inconstant billows：ever-moving waves.

17 Harfleur：an ancient seaport in northern France.

18 Grapple your minds to (the) sternage：fix your minds on the stern (船尾)，让想象追踪舰队而去。

19 as dead minnight still：as still (quiet) as the dead of night.

20 Guarded with：Guarded by.

21 not arrived to：not yet attaining. **pith and puissance**：full strength.

22—23 who is he … that will not follow：everyman … will follow. **but**：only. **enricht**(enriched)：adorned.

24 cull'd：hand-picked. **choice-drawn**：carefully chosen. **cavaliers**：骑士。

25 therein：in your thoughts.

27 girded：surrounded；besieged.

Suppose th' ambassador from the French comes back;
Tells Harry that the king doth offer him
Katharine his daughter; and with her, to dowry,
Some petty and unprofitable dukedoms.
The offer likes not: and the nimble gunner
With linstock now the devilish cannon touches,
[*Alarum, and chambers go off, within.*
And down goes all before them. Still be kind,
And eke out our performance with your mind.[*Exit.*

SCENE I

France. Before Harfleur.

Alarums. Enter KING HENRY, EXETER, BEDFORD, GLOSTER, *and* SOLDIERS, *with scaling-ladders.*

KING HENRY.

Once more unto the breach, dear friends, once more;
Or close the wall up with our English dead!
In peace there's nothing so becomes a man
As modest stillness and humility:
But when the blast of war blows in our ears,
Then imitate the action of the tiger;
Stiffen the sinews, summon up the blood,
Disguise fair nature with hard-favor'd rage:
Then lend the eye a terrible aspect;
Let it pry through the portage of the head
Like the brass cannon; let the brow o'erwhelm it
As fearfully as doth a galled rock
O'erhang and jutty his confounded base,
Swill'd with the wild and wasteful ocean.
Now set the teeth, and stretch the nostril wide;
Hold hard the breath, and bend up every spirit
To his full height! —On, on, you noble English,
Whose blood is fet from fathers of war-proof! —

29 **the king**：the French king.

30 **Katherine**：也作 Catherine，是 Henry VI 的幼女，当时 14 岁。 **to dowry**：as her dowry.

32 **likes**：pleases.

33 **linstock**：a long stick for lighting the cannon. **alarum**：noise of battle. **chambers**：small pieces of ordnance.

34 **Still**：always.

35 **eke out**：supplement. **mind**：imagination.

III.i

1 **unto**：rush into.

2 **close the wall up**：fill up the gap in the wall.

3 **becomes**：suits；befits.

4 **stillness**：staidness.

7 **summon up the blood**：work up your temper.

8 **Disguise**：cange（the appearance）. **fair nature**：your usual good-natured appearance. **hard-favor'd**：stern-faced；hard-featured.

9 **lend**：give；let（it）have. **aspect**：look；appearance.重音在第二音节。

10 **it**：the eye. **pry**：peer. **portage**：porthole；eye-sockets.

11 **o'erwhelm it**：overhang the eye.

12 **galled**：eroded by the waves.

13 **jutty**：jut over. **his confounded base**：its wornedaway foundation.

14 **Swill'd with**：swallowed by. **wasteful**：destructive.

16 **bend up**：srain to the utmost，like a bow. **spirit**：nerve.

17 **to his full height**：to its utmost（extent）.

18 **fet**：fetched. **of war-proof**：proved in war.

Fathers that, like so many Alexanders,
Have in these parts from morm till even fought,
And sheathed their swords for lack of argument:—
Dishonor not your mothers; now attest
That those whom you call'd fathers did beget you!
Be copy now to men of grosser blood,
And teach them how to war! —And you, good yeomen,
Whose limbs were made in England, show us here
The mettle of your pasture; let us swear
That you are worth your breeding: which I doubt not;
For there is none of you so mean and base,
That hath not nopble lustre in your eyes.
I see you stand like greyhounds in the slips,
Straining upon the start. The game's afoot:
Follow your spirit: and, upon this charge,
Cry 'God for Harry, England, and Saint George!'
[*Exeunt. Alarum, and chambers go off, within.*

SCENE II

The same.

Enter NYM, BARDOLPH, PISTOL, *and* BOY.

BARDOLPH.

On,on,on,on,on! to the breach, to the breach!

NYM.

Pray thee, corporal, stay: the knocks are too hot; and, for mine own part, I have not a case of lives: the humor of it is too hot, that it is the very plain-song of it.

PISTOL.

The plain-song is most just; for humors do abound;
Knocks go and come; God's vassals drop and die;
And sword and shield,
In bloody field,

19 **Alexanders**: men as brave as Alexander the great, the famous king of Macedon, who conquered Persia and Egypt.

20 **from morn till even**: from morning till evening.

21 **argument**: opposition.

22 **attest**: prove.

24 **copy**: example. **men of grosser blood**: 出身卑微的人。

25 **yeomen**: farmers,英国自耕农,是当时主要的兵源。

27 **The mettle of your pasture**: the quality of your background.

31 **in the slips**: on their leashes.

32 **Straining upon the start**: eager to begin the chase. **The game's afoot**: game 为一双关语:1. 猎物,在这意义上讲,本句相当于"Let's begin the chase"; 2. war game,在这意义上讲,本句相当于"Let's begin the action (battle)".

33 **Follow your spirit**: do what is in your nature to do; do what you are capable of doing. **upon this charge**: when you charge at the enemy.

34 **Cry**: give the war cry. **'God for Harry, England, and Saint George'**: God be in favor of Harry, England, and Saint George (the Patron saint of England).

III.ii

2 **the knocks are too hot**: the onset (onrush; impact) is too heady (precipitous).

3 **mine**: my (formerly used before a word beginning with a vowel or 'h'). **case**: set; pair. **humor**: temperament. **it**: the charge.

4 **plain-song**: simple tune, therefore, simple truth.

6 **God's vassals**: people; men.

Doth win immortal fame.

BOY.

Would I were in an alehouse in London! I would give all my fame for a pot of ale and safety.

PISTOL.

And I:

If wishes would prevail with me,
My purpose should not fail with me,
But thither would I hie.

BOY.

As duly, but not as truly,
As bird doth sing on bough.

Enter FLUELLEN.

FLUELLEN.

Got's plood! — Up to the preaches, you rascals! will you not up to the preaches? [*Driving them forward*.

PISTOL.

Be merciful, great duke, to men of mould!
Abate thy rage, abate thy manly rage!
Abate thy rage, great duke!
Good bawcock, bate thy rage! use lenity, sweet chuck!

NYM.

These be good humors! — your honor runs bad humors.

[*Exeunt* NYM, BARDOLPH, *and* PISTOL *driven in by* FLUELLEN.

BOY.

As young as I am, I have observed these three swashers. I am boy to them all three: but all they three, though they would serve me, could not be man to me; for, indeed, three such antics do not amount to a man. For Bardolph, — he is white-liver'd and red-faced; by the means whereof a' faces it out, but fights not. For Pistol, — he hath a killing tongue and a quiet sword; by the means whereof a' breaks words, and keeps whole weapons. For Nym, — he hath heard that men of few words are the best men;

10 **alehouse**：啤酒店。

13 **prevail**：avail；have effect.

15 **thither**：i.e.，to the battlefield. **hie**：hurry.

16 **duly**：properly；bound by duty. **truly**：naturally；in accord with one's bent.

18 **Got's plood**：God's blood（a mild oath）. Being a Welsh，Fluellen has an accent when speaking English. **preaches**：breaches.

19 **up to**：go（rush）up to.

20 **great duke**：an oath. **men of mould**：men of common clay.

23 **bawcock**：fine fellow，a term of endearment（from French 'beau coq'，meaning 'beautiful cock'）. **use lenity**：be merciful. **chuck**：chick（another term of endearment）.在本剧中 Pistol 常用一些法文字。

24 **good humors**：good fun. **runs bad humors**：has a bad temper.（humor 一字在莎士比亚时代的英国十分流行，为莎士比亚所讥讽，在本剧中 Nym 把这字作为口头禅，到处乱用。）

25 **swashers**：swashbucklers；phonies.

26 **boy**：servant. **though**：even if.

27 **man**：双关语 1. servant；2. manly man.

28 **antics**：clowns. **For**：as for.

29 **white-liver'd**：cowardly. **red-faced**：bluffy. **whereof**：of which.

30 **a'**：he. **faces it out**：brazens it out.

and therefore he scorns to say his prayers, lest a'should be thought a coward: but his few bad words are matcht with as few good deeds; for a' never broke any man's head but his own, and that was against a post when he was drunk. They will steal any thing, and call it purchase. Bardolph stole a lute-case, bore it twelve leagues, and sold it for three half-pence. Nym and Bardolph are sworn brothers in filching; and in Calais they stole a fire-shovel: I knew by that piece of service the men would carry coals. They would have me as familiar with men's pockets as their gloves or their handkerchers: which makes much against my manhood, if I should take from another's pocket to put into mine; for it is plain pocketing-up of wrongs. I must leave them, and seek some better service: their villainy goes against my weak stomach, and therefore I must cast it up. [*Exit*.

Enter FLUELLEN, GOWER *following*.

GOWER.

Captain Fluellen, you must come presently to the mines; the Duke of Gloster would speak with you.

FLUELLEN.

To the mines! tell you the duke, it is not so goot to come to the mines; for, look you, the mines is not according to the disciplines of the war: the concavities of it is not sufficient; for, look you, th' athversary — you may discuss unto the duke, look you — is digt himself four yard under the countermines: by Cheshu, I think a' will plow up all, if there is not petter directions.

GOWER.

The Duke of Gloster, to whom the order of the siege is given, is altogether directed by an Irishman, — a very valiant gentleman, i'faith.

FLUELLEN.

It is Captain Macmorris, is it not?

37 **post**：lamp-post or door-post.

38 **purchase**：booty (thieves' word).

43 **carry coals**：do any dirty work，和上文 fire-shovel 相联系。

43—44 **as familiar with men's pockets as their gloves or their handkerchers**：i.e.，to get my hand into and out of people's pockets (pick pockets) as freely as if I were their glovers or handkerchiefs.

45 **makes much against my manhood**：hurts much my pride.

46—47 **pocketing-up of wrongs**：putting up with affronts.

48—49 **weak stomach**：喻 tender conscience.

49 **cast it up**：throw it up，把它吐出来。

50 **mines**：tunnels.

52 **tell you the duke**：(you) tell the duke (the Duke of Gloster). **goot**：good.

54 **disciplines**：regular practices.

55 **th' athversary**：the adversary；the enemy.

56 **discuss**：declare；tell.

56—57 **is digt himself…countermines**：has dug countermines for four yards under our own mines.

57 **Cheshu**：Jesus.

58 **plow**：blow. **petter**：better.

59 **Duke of Gloster** (Gloucester)，名 Humphrey，是 Henry V 幼弟，指挥炮兵和工兵。

61 **i'faith**：in faith (a solemn declaration).

GOWER.

I think it be.

FLUELLEN.

By Cheshu, he is an ass, as in the 'orld: I will verify as much in his peard: he has no more directions in the true disciplines of the wars, look you, of the Roman disciplines, than is a puppy-dog.

GOWER.

Here a' comes; and the Scots captain, Captain Jamy, with him.

FLUELLEN.

Captain Jamy is a marvellous falorous gentleman, that is certain; and of great expedition and knowledge in th'auncient wars, upon my particular knowledge of his directions: by Cheshu, he will maintain his argument as well as any military man in the 'orld, in the disciplines of the pristine wars of the Romans.

Enter MACMORRIS *and* JAMY.

JAMY.

I say gude-day, Captain Fluellen.

FLUELLEN.

Got-den to your worship, goot Captain Jamy.

GOWER.

How now, Captain Macmorris! have you quit the mines? have the pioners given o'er?

MACMORRIS.

By Chrish, la, tish ill done; the work ish give over, the trompet sound the retreat. By my hand, I swear, and my father's soul, the work ish ill done; it ish give over: I would have blow'd up the town, so Chrish save me, la, in an hour: O, tish ill done, tish ill done; by my hand, tish ill done!

FLUELLEN.

Captain Macmorris, I peseech you now, will you vout-

64 he is an ass, as in the 'orld: he is as big a fool as there is in the world.

64—65 I will verify as much in his peard (beard): I will say as much to his face.

65 directions: capacity for directing; knowledge.

68 Scots: Scotch.

70 falorous: valorous.

71 expedition: a blunder between 'experience' and 'erudition'. **auncient**: ancient.

75 pristine: early.

76 这时场上四人,Gower 英格兰人,Fluellen 威尔士人,Jamy 苏格兰人,Macmorris 爱尔兰人,象征英国四民族的团结。 **gude-day**: good day.

77 Got-den: good evening. **your worship**: your honor.

79 pioners: pioneers, miners (constructors of earthworks). **given o'er**: given up.

80 By Chrish: by Christ (am oath). **la**: an exclamation to call attention to an emphatic statement. **tish**: it is. **ish**: is. **give over**: given over.

81 trompet: trumpet.

83 blow'd: blown.

86 peseech: beseech.

safe me, look you, a few disputations with you, as partly touching or concerning the disciplines of the war, the Roman wars, in the way of argument, look you, and friendly communication; partly to satisfy my opinion, and partly for the satisfaction, look you, of my mind, as touching the direction of the military discipline; that is the point.

JAMY.

It sall be vary gude, gude feith, gude captains baith: and I sall quit you with gude leve, as I may pick occasion; that sall I, marry.

MACMORRIS.

It is no time to discourse, so Chrish save me: the day is hot, and the weather, and the wars, and the king, and the dukes: it is no time to discourse. The town is beseecht, and the trompet call us to the breach; and we talk, and, be Chrish, do nothing: 'tis shame for us all: so God sa' me, 'tis shame to stand still; it is shame, by my hand: and there is throats to be cut, and works to be done; and there ish nothing done, so Chrish sa' me, la.

JAMY.

By the mess, ere theise eyes of mine take themselves to slomber, ay 'll de gude service, or ay 'll lig i' th' grund for it; ay, or go to death; and ay 'll pay 't as valorously as I may, that sall I suerly do, that is the breff and the long. Marry, I wad full fain heard some question 'tween you tway.

FLUELLEN.

Captain Macmorris, I think, look you, under your correction, there is not many of your nation —

MACMORRIS.

Of my nation! What ish my nation? Ish a villain, and a bastard, and a knave, and a rascal. What ish my

86—87 voutsafe: vouchsafe; allow.

87 disputations: words.

94 sall: shall. **vary gude**: very good. **gude feith**: in good faith; really. **baith**: both.

95 quit you: answer you. **with gude leve**: with your kind permission.

96 marry: by the Virgin Mary (a mild oath).

97—99 perhaps he means that the weather, the wars, the king and the dukes are all very hot.

100 beseecht: besieged.

101 be Chrish: by Christ.

102 God sa' me: god save me.

106 by the mess: by the mass (a mild oath). **ere**: before. **theise**: these.

107 slomber: slumber. **ay 'll**: I'll. **de**: do. **lig**: lie.

107—108 i' th' grund: in the ground.

108 pay't: pay for it (with my death).

109 suerly: surely.

110 breff: brief; short.他想说 that is the long and the short of it. **I wad full fain**: I would gladly have.

111 tway: two.

112—113 under your correction: correct me if I am wrong.

114 Macmorris is plainly offended because he thinks Fluellen (a Welsh) is going to speak disparagingly of his nation (the scots) which he is jealously proud of. (Ish: 'It's' or rather 'Is it') nation? Who talks of my nation?

FLUELLEN.

Look you, if you take the matter otherwise than is meant, Captain Macmorris, peradventure I shall think you do not use me with that affability as in discretion you ought to use me, look you; being as goot a man as yourself, both in the disciplines of war, and in the derivation of my birth, and in other particularities.

MCMORRIS.

I do not know you so good a man as myself: so Chrish save me, I will cut off your head.

GOWER.

Gentlemen both, you will mistake each other.

JAMY.

A! that's a foul fault. [*A parley sounded.*

GOWER.

The town sounds a parley.

FLUELLEN.

Captain Macmorris, when there is more petter opportunity to be required, look you, I will be so pold as to tell you I know the disciplines of war; and there is an end.

[*Exeunt.*

SCENE III

The same.

The GOVERNOR *and some* CITIZENS *on the walls; the English forces below. Enter* KING HENRY *and his* TRAIN *before the Gates.*

KING HENRY.

How yet resolves the governor of the town?
This is the latest parle we will admit:
Therefore, to our best mercy give yourselves;
Or, like to men proud of destruction,

118 **peradventure**: perhaps.

119 **use**: treat.

125 **you will mistake each other**: you seem to be determined to misunderstand each other.

126 **parley**: call by drum or trumpet for discussion of terms for armistice.

128 **petter**: better.

129 **required**: acquired. **pold**: bold.

III.iii

1 Has the governor of the town come to some decision yet?

2 **the latest parle**: the last parley (armistice negotiation).

3 **to our best mercy give yourselves**: avail yourselves of our best mercy.

4 **like to**: like. **proud of destruction**: elated at the thought of death.

Defy us to our worst: for, as I am a soldier,
A name that, in my thoughts, becomes me best,
If I begin the battery once again,
I will not leave the lalf-achieved Harfleur
Till in her ashes she lie buried.
The gates of mercy shall be all shut up;
And the flesht soldier,—rough and hard of heart,—
In liberty of bloody hand shall range
With conscience wide as hell; mowing like grass
Your fresh-fair virgins and your flowering infants.
What is it then to me, if impious war,—
Array'd in flames, like to the prince of fiends,—
Do, with his smircht complexion, all fell feats
Enlinkt to waste and desolation?
What is 't to me, when you yourselves are cause,
If your pure maidens fall into the hand
Of hot and forcing violation?
What rein can hold licentious wickedness
When down the hill he holds his fierce career?
We may as bootless spend our vain command
Upon th' enraged soldiers in their spoil,
As send precepts to the leviathan
To come ashore. Therefore, you men of Harfleur
Take pity of your town and of your people,
Whiles yet my soldiers are in my command;
Whiles yet the cool and temperate wind of grace
O'erblows the filthy and contagious clouds
Of heady murder, spoil, and villainy.
If not, why, in a moment, look to see
The blind and bloody soldier with foul hand
Defile the locks of your shrill-shrieking daughters;
Your fathers taken by the silver beards,
And their most reverend heads dasht to the walls;
Your naked infants spitted upon pikes,

7 **battery**：attack；assault.

8 **half-achieved**：half-won.

11 **flesht**：(like a hound) hardened by the taste of flesh.见 II iv 50.

12 **In** (the) **liberty…range**：shall pillage with a free hand.

13 **wide**：indifferent. **as hell**：extremely.

14 **fresh-fair**：fresh and fair.

17—18 **all fell feats…desolation**：all the cruel acts associated with the sacking of cities.

21 **violation**：rape.

23 **he**：it,指上行的 licentious wickedness,在这里把它比作一匹马。 **career**：short gallop at full speed.

24 **bootless**：vainly. **spend**：waste.

25 **spoil**：plundering；ravaging.

26 **precepts**：重音在第二音节,written commands. **leviathan**：huge sea monster,见《圣经·旧约·诗篇》104 篇 26 节。

28 **of**：on.

30 **grace**：mercy.

31 **O'erblows**：blows over；prevails over.

32 **heady**：violent；headstrong.

34 **blind**：reckless；indiscriminate.

35 **locks**：hair.

38 **spitted**：pierced through by and fixed.

Whiles the mad mothers with their howls confused
Do break the clouds, as did the wives of Jewry
At Herod's bloody-hunting slaughtermen.
What say you? will you yield, and this avoid?
Or, guilty in defense, be thus destroy'd?

GOVERNOR OF HARFLEUR.

Our expectation hath this day an end:
The Dauphin, whom of succors we entreated,
Returns us, that his powers are yet not ready
To raise so great a siege. Therefore, dread king,
We yield our town and lives to thy soft mercy.
Enter our gates; dispose of us and ours;
For we no longer are defensible.

KING HENRY.

Open your gates. —Come, uncle Exeter,
Go you and enter Harfleur; there remanin,
And fortify it strongly 'gainst the French:
Use mercy to them all. For us, dear uncle,—
The winter coming on, and sickness growing
Upon our soldiers,—we will retire to Calais.
To-night in Harfleur will we be your guest;
To-morrow for the march are we addrest.

[*Flourish, The king and his train enter the town.*

SCENE IV

The French KING's *palace.*

Enter KATHARINE *and* ALICE.

KATHARINE.

Alice, tu as été en Angleterre, et tu parles bien le langage.

ALICE.

Un peu, madame.

KATHARINE.

40 **break**: pierce. **Jewry**: Judea,犹太。

41 **Herod's bloody-hunting slaughtermen**: 指犹太国王希律(37—4 B.C.)为了除灭耶稣而将伯利恒城里以及四境两岁以内的男婴杀尽一事,见《圣经·新约·马太福音》2 章 16 节。

43 **defense**: resistance.

44 **our expectation**: i.e. our hope of being rescued.

45 **Dauphin**: 法国王太子,见 I. ii 236. **of**: concerning.

46 **Returns us**: sends word back to us. **powers**: troops.

47 **dread**: dreadful; revered.

48 **soft**: tender.

50 **defensible**: capable of defending ourselves.

54 **Use**: show. **For us**: as for me.

58 **addrest**: prepared.

III.iv

1 Alice, you have been to England and you speak well the language.

2 A little, madam.

Je te prie, m'enseignez; il faut que j'apprenne à parler. Comment appelez-vous la main en Anglois?

ALICE.

La main? elle est appelée de hand.

KATHARINE.

De hand. *Et les doigts?*

ALICE.

Les doigts? ma foi, j'oublie les doigts; mais je me souviendrai. Les doigts? je pense qu'ils sont appelés de fingres; *oui*, de fingres.

KATHARINE.

La main, de hand; *les doigts*, de fingres. *Je pense que je suis le bon écolier; j'ai gagné deux mots d'Anglois vîtement. Comment appelez-vous les ongles?*

ALICE.

Les ongles? nous les appelons de nails.

KATHARINE.

De nails. *Ecoutez; dites-moi, si je parle bien*: de hand, de fingres, *et* de nails.

ALICE.

C'est bien dit, madame; il est fort bon Anglois.

KATHARINE.

Dites-moi l'Anglois pour le bras.

ALICE.

De arm, *madame*.

KATHARINE.

Et le coude?

ALICE.

D'elbow.

KATHARINE.

D'elbow. *Je m'en fais la répétition de tous les mots que vous m'avez appris dès à présent.*

ALICE.

Il est trop difficile, madame, comme je pense.

3—4 I beg you to teach me; I'll have to learn to speak (it). How do you call 'la main' in English?

5 La main? It is called hand.

6 Hand. And 'les doigts'?

7—9 Les doigts? really, I've fotgotten how they are called; but I shall bring them back to memory. Les doigts? I think they are called 'fingres'; yes, fingres.

10—12 **Je pense … ongles?**: I think I am a good pupil; I have learned two English words quickly. How do you call 'les ongles'?

13 Les ongles? We call them 'nails'.

14—15 Nails. Listen; tell me whether I speak right: hand, fingres, and nails.

16 It's well said, madam; it is quite good English.

17 Tell me the English for 'le bras'.

18 Arm, madam.

19 And 'le coude'?

20 Elbow.

21—22 Elbow. I'll repeat all the words you have taught me up to now.

23 It is too difficult, madam, in my view.

KATHARINE.

Excusez-moi, *Alice*; *écoutez*: d'hand, de fingres, de nails, d'arm, de bibow.

ALICE.

D'elbow, *madame*.

KATHARINE.

O Seigneur Dieu, *je m'en oublie*! d'elbow. *Comment appelez-vous le col*?

ALICE.

De neck, *madame*.

KATHARINE.

De nick. *Et le menton*?

ALICE.

De chin.

KATHARINE.

De sin. *Le col*, de nick; *le menton*, de sin.

ALICE.

Oui. *Sauf votre honneur*, *en vérité*, *vous prononcez les mots aussi droit que les natifs d'Angleterre*.

KATHARINE.

Je ne doute point d'apprendre, *par la grace de Dieu*, *et en peu de temps*.

ALICE.

N'avez-vous pas déjà oublié ce que je vous ai enseigné?

KATHARINE.

Non, *je réciterai à vous promptement*: d'hand, de fingres, de mails,—

ALICE.

De nails, *madame*.

KATHARINE.

De nails, de arm, de ilbow.

ALICE.

Sauf votre honneur, d'elbow.

KATHARINE.

24—25 Excuse me, Alice; listen: hand, fingres, nails, arm, bilbow.

26 Elbow, madam.

27—28 O Lord God, I forgot it! elbow. How do you call 'le col'?

29 Neck, madam.

30 Nick (裂口). And 'le menton'?

31 Chin.

32 Sin (罪孽). Le col, nick; le menton, sin.

33—34 Yes, save your honor, in truth you pronounce these words as correctly as the natives of England.

35—36 I don't doubt at all to learn (them) by the grace of God, and in no time, too.

37 Haven't you already forgotten what I have taught you?

38—39 No, I shall recite to you promptly: hand, fingers, mails,—

40 Nails, madam.

41 Nails, arm, ilbow.

42 Save your honor, elbow.

Ainsi dis-je; d'elbow, de nick, *et* de sin. *Comment appelez-vous le pied et la robe?*

ALICE.

De foot, *madame*; *et* de coun.

KATHARINE.

De foot *et* de coun! *O Seigneur Dieu! ce sont mots de son mauvais, corruptible, gros, et impudique, et non pour les dames d'honneur d'user: je ne voudrais prononcer ces mots devant les seigneurs de France pour tout le monde. Foh! le* foot *et le* coun! *Néanmoins, je réciterai une autre fois ma leçon ensemble*: d'hand, de fingres, de nails, d'arm, d'elbow, de nick, de sin, de foot, de coun.

ALICE.

Excellent, madame!

KATHARINE.

C'est assez pour une fois: allons-nous à diner. [*Exeunt.*

SCENE V

The same.

Enter the KING OF FRANCE, *the* DAUPHIN, BOURBON, *the* CONSTABLE OF FRANCE, *and others.*

FRENCH KING.

'Tis certain he hath past the river Somme.

THE CONSTABLE OF FRANCE.

And if he be not fought withal, my lord,
Let us not live in France; let us quit all,
And give our vineyards to a barbarous people.

DAUPHIN.

O Dieu vivant! shall a few sprays of us,
The emptying of our fathers' luxury,
Our scions, put in wild and savage stock,
Spirt up so suddenly into the clouds,

43—44 Thus I say; elbow, nick, and sin. How do you call 'le pied' and 'la robe'?

45 Foot, madam; and coun (a mistake for 'gown').

46—52 Foot and coun. (法语里 foot 音近 foutre：fuck，coun 意为 cunt，阴户。)O Lord God! These two are words of bad sound, corruptible, gross, and indecent, and are not to be used by honorable ladies; I wouldn't for all the world pronounce these words in the presence of the lords of France. Pooth, foot and coun! Nevertheless, I'll repeat once more my whole lesson: hand, fingres, nails, arm, elbow, nick, sin, foot, coun.

54 That's enough for one time, let's go to dinner.

III.v

1 **past the river Somme**：英军从 Harfleur 北撤往 Calais，必须过 Somme 河，而法军已将下游桥梁尽拆。疲惫的英军只好沿河向东，寻找可涉水渡河之处，终于在 Nesle 过河。

2 **fought withal**：fought against; resisted.

5 **O Dieu vivant**：by the living God. **sprays**：drops of semen.

And overlook their grafters?

DUKE OF BOURBON.

Normans, but bastard Normans, Norman bastards!
Mort de ma vie! if they march along
Unfought withal, but I will sell my dukedom,
To buy a slobbery and a dirty farm
In that nook-shotten isle of Albion.

THE CONSTABLE OF FRANCE.

Dieu de batailles! where have they this mettle?
Is not their climate foggy, raw, and dull;
On whom, as in despite, the sun looks pale,
Killing their fruit with frowns? Can sodden water,
A drench for sur-rein'd jades, their barley-broth,
Decoct their cold blood to such valiant heat?
And shall our quick blood, spirited with wine,
Seem frosty? O, for honor of our land,
Let us not hang like roping icicles
Upon our houses' thatch, whiles a more frosty people
Sweat drops of gallant youth in our rich fields,—
Poor we may call them in their native lords!

DAUPHIN.

By faith and honour,
Our madams mock at us, and plainly say
Our mettle is bred out, and they will give
Their bodies to the lust of English youth
To new-store France with bastard warriors.

DUKE OF BOURBON.

They bid us to the English dancing-schools,
And teach lavoltas high and swift corantos;
Saying our grace is only in our heels,
And that we are most lofty runaways.

FRENCH KING.

Where is Montjoy the herald? speed him hence;
Let him greet England with our sharp defiance.—

5—9 此段指 1066 年诺曼底的威廉征服英国后，英国人里有法国人的血统。

6 **emptying**: outflow; issue. **luxury**: lust.

7 **scions**: shoots，嫁接时优种的枝条。 **put in**: grafted on. **savage**: uncultivated. **stock**: 砧木。

8 **Spirt up**: Shoot up.

9 **overlook**: look down on. **grafters**: original trees from which the scions were taken，接枝的母本。

10 **but**: only.

11 **Mort de ma vie**: (French) death of my life. vie 读作两音节。

12 **but I will**: if I will not.

13 **slobbery**: sloppy; muddy.

14 **nook-shotten**: thrust into a corner; inaccessible. **Albion**: 古英格兰的名称，原意"白色国土"，从多佛白垩削壁得名。

15 **Dieu de batailles**: (French) God of battles. batailles 读作三音节。 **where have they** 后省 got. **mettle**: courage.

17 **in despite**: out of ill will; spitefully.

18 **sodden** (past participle of 'seethe'): boiled.

19 **drench**: a large draught, especially for a sick animal. **surrein'd**: overridden. **barley-broth**: 大麦汤，指英国人的淡色啤酒 ale (used in treating horses).

20 **Decoct**: warm up; boil.

21 **spirited**: animated. **wine**: 葡萄酒。

22 **honor**: 前省略 the.

23 **roping**: dangling.

24 **whiles**: while.

25 **drops**: drops of blood.

26 We may call them (rich fields) 'poor' in their native lords (owners).

29 **bred out**: exhausted.

31 **new-store**: stock again.

33 **And**: to. **lavoltas**: leaping dances. **corantos**: dances with quick-gliding or running steps.

34 **Saying**: 后省略 that. **grace**: virtue; worth.

35 **lofty**: haughty.

36 **speed**: hasten.

Up, princes! and, with spirit of honor edged
More sharper than your swords, hie to the field:
Charles Delabreth, high-Constable of France;
You Dukes of Orleans, Bourbon, and of Berri,
Alençon, Brabant, Bar, and Burgundy;
Jaques Chatillon, Rambures, Vaudemont,
Beaumont, Grandpré, Roussi, and Fauconberg,
Foix, Lestrale, Bouciqualt, and Charolois;
High dukes, great princes, barons, lords, and knights,
For your great seats now quit you of great shames.
Bar Harry England, that sweeps through our land
With pennons painted in the blood of Harfleur:
Rush on his host, as doth the melted snow
Upon the valleys, whose low vassal seat
The Alps doth spit and void his rheum upon:
Go down upon him,—you have power enough,—
And in a captive chariot into Rouen
Bring him our prisoner.

THE CONSTABLE OF FRANCE.

This becomes the great.
Sorry am I his numbers are so few,
His soldiers sick, and famisht in their march;
For I am sure, when he shall see our army,
He 'll drop his heart into the sink of fear,
And for achievement offer us his ransom.

FRENCH KING.

Therefore, lord Constable, haste on Montjoy;
And let him say to England, that we send
To know what willling ransom he will give.—
Prince Dauphin, you shall stay with us in Rouen.

DAUPHIN.

Not so, I do beseech your majesty.

FRENCH KING.

Be patient; for you shall remain with us.

38 **up**: rouse up. **edged**: sharpened.

39 **More sharper**: to strengthen a comparative by means of adding 'more' to it was a common practice. **hie**: hasten.

47 **seats**: estates; holdings. **quit you**: rid yourselves.

48 **Bar**: stop. **Harry England**: Henry V of England.

49 **pennons**: banners.

50 **host**: army.

51 **vassal**: base.

52 **void his rheum**: spit its phlegm,吐痰。

54 **captive chariot**: 囚车。

56 **his**: Henry V's.

57 **famisht**: famished.

59 **sink**: 落水洞。

60 **for achievement**: instead of fighting to victory.

62 **England**: King of England.

Now forth, lord Constable, and princes all,
And quickly bring us word of England's fall. [*Exeunt*.

SCENE VI

The English camp in Picardy.

Enter GOWER *and* FLUELLEN, *meeting*.

GOWER.

How now, Captain Fluellen! come you from the bridge?

FLUELLEN.

I assure you, there is very excellent services committed at the pridge.

GOWER.

Is the Duke of Exeter safe?

FLUELLEN.

The Duke of Exeter is as magnanimous as Agamemnon; and a man that I love and honor with my soul, and my heart, and my duty, and my life, and my living, and my uttermost power: he is not — Got be praised and plest! — any hurt in the 'orld; but keeps the pridge most valiantly, with excellent discipline. There is an auncient there at the pridge, — I think in my very conscience he is as valiant a man as Mark Antony; and he is a man of no estimation in the 'orld; but I did see him do gallant service.

GOWER.

What do you call him?

FLUELLEN.

He is called Auncient Pistol.

GOWER.

I know him not.

FLUELLEN.

Here is the man.

67 **forth**：go forth.

III.vi

1 **bridge**：指 Ternoise 小河上的桥。

3 **pridge**：bridge.

5 **magnanimous**：of great courage. **Agamemnon**：迈西尼国王，进攻特洛伊的希腊军队的统帅，见荷马史诗《伊利亚德》。

8 **Got**：God. **plest**：blessed.

9 **any**：in any degree.

10 **discipline**：military experience. **auncient**：ancient；ensign，少尉军旗官。

12 **Mark Antony**（Marcus Antonius，around 82—30 B.C.）：Roman general，well-known for bravery.

13 **estimatin**：reputation.

Enter PISTOL

PISTOL.

Captain, I thee beseech to do me favors:
The Duke of Exeter doth love thee well.

FLUELLEN.

Ay, I praise Got; and I have merited some love at his hands.

PISTOL.

Bardolph, a soldier, firm and sound of heart,
And of buxom valor, hath, by cruel fate,
And giddy Fortune's furious fickle wheel,—
That goddess blind,
That stands upon the rolling restless stone,—

FLUELLEN.

By your patience, Auncient Pistol. Fortune is painted plind, with a muffler afore her eyes, to signify to you that Fortune is plind; and she is painted also with a wheel, to signify to you, which is the moral of it, that she is turning, and inconstant, and mutability, and variation: and her foot, look you, is fixt upon a spherical stone, which rolls, and rolls, and rolls: —in good truth, the poet makes a most excellent description of it: Fortune is an excellent moral.

PISTOL.

Fortune is Bardolph's foe, and frowns on him;
For he hath stoln a pax, and hanged must a'be,—
A damned death!
Let gallows gape for dog; let man go free,
And let not hemp his windpipe suffocate:
But Exeter hath given the doom of death
For pax of little price.
Therefore, go speak,—the duke will hear thy voice;
And let not Bardolph's vital thread be cut
With edge of penny cord and vile reproach:

24 **buxom**: lively.

25—27 这里和下文,描写中世纪“命运女神”的通俗形象。

28 **patience**: indulgence; permission.

29 **afore**: in front of.

30 **plind**: blind.

31 **moral**: hidden meaning.

35—36 **is an excellent moral**: reads us an excellent lesson.

38 **stoln**: stolen. **pax**: 天主教教堂里刻有耶稣钉十字架的铜版画牌,为教士和信徒亲吻用。

41 **hemp**: 麻绳;绞索。

42 **doom**: sentence.

45 **vital thread**: life-line.

Speak, captain, for his life, and I will thee requite.

FLUELLEN.

Auncient Pistol, I do partly understand your meaning.

PISTOL.

Why, then, rejoice therefore.

FLUELLEN.

Certainly, auncient, it is not a thing to rejoice at: for if, look you, he were my prother, I would desire the duke to use his goot pleasure, and put him to execution; for discipline ought to be used.

PISTOL.

Die and be damn'd! and figo for thy friendship!

FLUELLEN.

It is well.

PISTOL.

The fig of Spain! [*Exit*.

FLUELLEN.

Very goot.

GOWER.

Why, this is an arrant counterfeit rascal; I remember him now; a bawd, a cutpurse.

FLUELLEN.

I'll assure you, a'utter'd as prave 'ords at the pridge as you shall see in a summer's day. But it is very well; what he has spoke to me, that is well, I warrant you, when time is serve.

GOWER.

Why, 'tis a gull, a fool, a rogue, that now and then goes to the wars, to grace himself, at his return into London, under the form of a soldier. And such fellows are perfect in the great commanders' names: and they will learn you by rote where services were done; — at such and such a sconce, at such a breach, at such a convoy; who came off bravely, who was shot, who disgraced, what terms the

47 requite: repay.

52 use his goot(d) **pleasure**: do as he wishes.

53 used: enforced.

54 figo: Spanish for 'fig', a word often used contemptuously, 意思是"毫无价值之物"。

56 fig of Spain: 表轻蔑的手势,把拇指夹在食指和中指中间,或塞在口里,相当于"操你的"。

58 arrant: out-and-out. **counterfeit**: deceitful; false.

59 cutpurse: pickpocket.

60—61 as you shall see in a summer's day: 谚语性口头禅。

62 spoke: spoken.

62—63 when time is serve: when time is opportune, 参看 II. i 5

64 gull: dupe; fool.

65 grace: confer honor on.

66 perfect: letter perfect; thoroughly learned.

67—68 learn you by rote: learn by rote; memorize. ('you', a dative, is an idiomatic use, implying the person addressed is incidentally interested.)

68 services: military feats.

69 sconce: bulwark; earthwork.

70 terms: conditions.

enemy stood on; and this they con perfectly in the phrase of war, which they trick up with new-turn'd oaths: and what a beard of the general's cut, and a horrid suit of the camp, will do among foaming bottles and ale-washt wits, is wonderful to be thought on. But you must learn to know such slanders of the age, or else you may be marvellously mistook.

FLUELLEN.

I tell you what, Captain Gower; — I do perceive he is not the man that he would glady make show to the 'orld he is: if I find a hole in his coat, I will tell him my mind. [*Drum within*.] Hark you, the king is coming; and I must speak with him from the pridge.

Drum and colors. Enter KING HENRY, GLOSTER, *and his poor* SOLDIERS. Got pless your majesty!

KING HENRY.

How now, Fluellen! camest thou from the bridge?

FLUELLEN.

Ay, so please your majesty. The Duke of Exeter has very gallantly maintain'd the pridge: the French is gone off, look you; and there is gallant and most prave passages: marry, th' athversary was have possession of the pridge; but he is enforced to retire, and the Duke of Exeter is master of the pridge: I can tell your majesty, the duke is a prave man.

KING HENRY.

What men have you lost, Fluellen?

FLUELLEN.

The perdition of th' athversary hath been very great, reasonable great: marry, for my part, I think the duke hath lost never a man, but one that is like to be executed for robbing a church, — one Bardolph, if your majesty know the man: his face is all bubukles, and whelks, and knobs, and flames o' fire: and his lips plows at

71 **con**: know; learn by heart.

72 **trick up**: deck out; adorn. **new-turn'd**: newly coined.

73—75 **what a beard … wits**: 为一主语从句,其中 a beard of the general's cut (a beard cut in a fashion like that of the general) 和 a horrid suit of the camp 为主语,will do 为谓语,what 是宾语。

76 **slanders of the age**: slanderers of the age; abusers of our time.

77 **marvellously**: grievously. **mistook** (**mistaken**): taken in; led astray.

79—80 **make show … he is**: make the world believe he is.

80 **find a hole in his coat**: find some fault in him.

81 **Hark you**: Listen.

82 **from the pridge**: about the bridge.

85 **so please**: if it pleases.

86 **maintain'd**: defended. **is gone off**: has gone away. Passive voice was used with some verbs of motion.

87—88 **passages**: actions.

88 **th' athversary**: the adversary; the enemy. **was have**: had.

89 **enforced**: forced. **retire**: retreat.

93 **perdition**: loss of life.

94 **reasonable**: reasonably.

95 **like to be**: on the point of being.

97 **bubuckles**: mixture of 'bubo' (沟腺炎) and 'carbuncle' (痈)。**whelks**: red pimples.

98 **knobs**: pimples. **plows**: blows. **it**: the nose.

his nose, and it is like a coal of fire, sometimes plue and sometimes red; but his nose is executed, and his fire's out.

KING HENRY.

We would have all such offenders so cut off, and we give express charge that in our marches through the country, there be nothing compelled from the villages, nothing taken but paid for, none of the French upbraided or abused in disdainful language; for when lenity and cruelty play for a kingdom, the gentler gamester is the soonest winner.

Tucket. Enter MONTJOY

MONTJOY.

You know me by my habit.

KING HENRY.

Well, then, I know thee: what shall I know of thee?

MONTJOY.

My master's mind.

KING HENRY.

Unfold it.

MONTJOY.

Thus says my king: — Say thou to Harry of England: Though we seem'd dead, we did but sleep: advantage is a better soldier than rashness. Tell him, we could have rebuked him at Harfleur, but that we thought not good to bruise an injury till it were full ripe: — now we speak upon our cue, and our voice is imperial: England shall repent his folly, see his weakness, and admire our sufferance. Bid him, therefore, consider of his ransom; which must proportion the losse we have borne, the subjects we have lost, the disgrace we have digested; which, in weight to reanswer, his pettiness would bow under. For our losses, his exchequer is too poor; for th'effusion of our blood, the muster of his kingdom too

100 **executed**: slit (before being hanged).

101 **out**: extinguished.

104 **compelled**: taken by force.

106 **lenity**: leniency.

107 **play for**: gamble for. **gamester**: gambler.

108 **Tucket**: sound of a trumpet.

109 **habit**: dress.他是 herald,有专门的服饰,叫 tabard.

110 **of thee**: from you.

114 **did but sleep**: only slept. **advantage**: favorable opportunity.

116 **rebuked**: checked; repressed. **but**: only; except. thought 和 not 之间省略 it.

117 **injury**: boil; tumor.

118 **cue**: 舞台提词。 **upon our cue**: at the proper moment.

118—119 England shall: The King of England must.

119—120 **admire our sufferance**: wonder at our forbearance.

121 **proportion**: be in proportion to.

122 **have digested**: have stomached.

123 **to reanswer**: in order to compensate for. **his pettiness**: a man so weak (meaning Henry V).

123—124 **bow under**: bend down.

124 **For**: In order to compensate for, 下同。 **exchequer**: royal treasury.

125 **effusion**: shedding. **muster**: all the persons.

faint a number; and for our disgrace, his own person, knelling at our feet, but a weak and worthless satisfaction. To this add defiance: and tell him, for conclusion, he hath betray'd his folowers, whose condemnation is pronounced. So far my king and master; so much my office.

KING HENRY.

What is thy name? I know thy quality.

MONTJOY.

Montjoy.

KING HENRY.

Thou dost thy office fairly. Turn thee back,
And tell thy king, —I do not seek him now;
But could be willing to march on to Calais
Without impeachment: for, to say the sooth,—
Though 'tis no wisdom to confess so much
Unto an enemy of craft and vantage,—
My people are with sichness much enfeebled;
My numbers lessen'd; and those few I have,
Almost no better thatn so many French;
Who when they were in health, I tell thee, herald,
I thought upon one pair of English legs
Did march three Frenchmen.—Yet, forgive me, God,
That I do brag thus! —this your air of France
Hath blown that vice in me; I must repent.
Go, therefore, tell thy master here I am;
My ransom is this frail and worthless trunk;
My army but a weak and sickly guard:
Yet, God before, tell him we will come on,
Though France himself, and such another neighbor,
Stand in our way. There's for thy labor, Montjoy.

[*Gives a purse.*

Go, bid thy master well advise himself:
If we may pass, we will; if we be hinder'd,

126 **faint**：insignificant.此句省略动词 is，下句同。

131 **quality**：business；profession.

133 **fairly**：as you should.

135 **could**：would.

136 **impeachment**：hindrance,来源于法语 empêchement. **sooth**：truth.

138 **of craft and vantage**：who is not only clever，but also has the advantage.

146 **blown**：blown up；inflated. **that vice**：bragging.

148 **trunk**：body.

150 **God before**：before God.

153 **well advise himself**：think carefully.

We shall your tawny ground with your red blood
Discolor: and so, Montjoy, fare you well.
The sum of all our answer is but this:
We would not seek a battle, as we are;
Nor, as we are, we say, we will not shun it:
So tell your master.

MONTJOY.

I shall deliver so. Thanks to your highness. [*Exit*.

DUKE OF GLOSTER.

I hope they will not come upon us now.

KING HENRY.

We are in God's hand, brother, not in theirs.
March to the bridge; it now draws toward night:—
Beyond the river we'll encamp ourselves;
And on to-morrow bid them march away. [*Exeunt*.

SCENE VII

The French camp near Agincourt.

Enter the CONSTABLE OF FRANCE, *the* LORD RAMBURES, ORLEANS, *the* DAUPHIN, *and others*.

THE CONSTABLE OF FRANCE.

Tut! I have the best armor of the world. — Would it were day!

DUKE OF ORLEANS.

You have an excellent armor; but let my horse have his due.

THE CONSTABLE OF FRANCE.

It is the best horse of Europe.

DUKE OF ORLEANS.

Will it never be morning?

DAUPHIN.

My Lord of Orleans, and my lord high-Constable, you talk of horse and armor?

155 **tawny**: yellow.

156 **Discolor**: change the color of.

160 **so**: as you have said.

III.vii

1 **armor**: suit of mail.

DUKE OF ORLEANS.

You are as well provided of both as any prince in the world.

DAUPHIN.

What a long night is this! — I will not change my horse with any that treads but on four pasterns. *Ça, ha!* he bounds from the earth, as if his entrails were hairs; *le cheval volant*, the Pegasus, *qui a les narines de feu!* When I bestride him, I soar, I am a hawk: he trots the air; the earth sings when he touches it; the basest horn of his hoof is more musical than the pipe of Hermes.

DUKE OF ORLEANS.

He's of the color of the nutmeg.

DAUPHIN.

And of the heat of the ginger. It is a beast for Prseus: he is pure air and fire; and the dull elements of earth and water never appear in him, but only in patient stillness while his rider mounts him: he is, indeed, a horse; and all other jades you may call beasts.

THE CONSTABLE OF FRANCE.

Indeed, my lord, it is a most absolute and excellent horse.

DAUPHIN.

It is the prince of palfreys; his neigh is like the bidding of a monarch, and his countenance enforces homage.

DUKE OF ORLEANS.

No more, cousin.

DAUPHIN.

Nay, the man hath no wit that cannot, from the rising of the lark to the lodging of the lamb, vary deserved praise on my palfrey: it is a theme as fluent as the sea; turn the sands into eloquent tongues, and my horse is argument for them all: 'tis a subject for a sovereign to reason on, and for a sovereigh's sovereign to ride on; and for

9 provided of: provided with.

11 change: trade.

12 pasterns: feet; a pastern is that part of a horse's foot between the hoof and the fetlock. **Ça**: (French) there.

13 as if his entrails were hairs: as if he were stuffed with hair (like a tennis ball made in those days, which can bound very high).

13—14 le cheval volant: (French) the flying horse.

14 Pegasus: 希腊神话中有翼的天马。 **qui a les narines de feu**: (French) that has nostrils of fire.

17 the pipe of Hermes: the shepherd's pipe invented by Hermes. Hermes 为希腊神话中天神的使者。

18 nutmeg: 肉豆蔻。

19 of the heat of the ginger: as fiery as the taste of ginger. **Perseus**: 希腊传说中的英雄。

20—21 he is pure air…appear in him: 当时认为万物由四种元素构成:气、火、土、水。前两种轻,后两种重。

21 but: except.

23 jades: 驽马。

24 absolute: perfect.

26 palfreys: saddle horses.

29—30 rising of the lark: dawn (when the lark begins to soar in the sky).

30 lodging: lying down.

32—33 argument: a worthy subject.

the world, familiar to us and unknown, to lay apart their particular functions, and wonder at him. I once writ a sonnet in his praise, and began thus: 'Wonder of nature,'—

DUKE OF ORLEANS.

I have heard a sonnet begin so to one's mistress.

DAUPHIN.

Then did they imitate that which I composed to my courser; for my horse is my mistress.

DUKE OF ORLEANS.

Your mistress bears well.

DAUPHIN.

Me well; which is the prescript praise and perfection of a good and particular mistress.

THE CONSTABLE OF FRANCE.

Ma foi, methought yesterday your mistress shrewdly shook your back.

DAUPHIN.

So, perhaps, did yours.

THE CONSTABLE OF FRANCE.

Mine was not bridled.

DAUPHIN.

O, then, belike she was old and gentle; and you rode, like a kern of Ireland, your French hose off, and in your strait strossers.

THE CONSTABLE OF FRANCE.

You have good judgement in horsemanship.

DAUPHIN.

Be warn'd by me, then: they that ride so, and ride not warily, fall into foul bogs. I had rather have my horse to my mistress.

THE CONSTABLE OF FRANCE.

I had as lief have my mistress a jade.

DAUPHIN.

35 **and unknown**: or unknown.

36 **writ**: wrote.

43 **Me well**: Bears me well. **prescript**: prescribed; normal.

44 **particular**: special; belonging to me only.

45 **Ma foi**: (French) by my faith. **shrewdly**: intensely.

49 **belike**: perhaps; probably.

50 **kern of Ireland**: Irish foot soldier. **French hose**: baggy breeches,马裤。

51 **strait strossers**: tight-fitting trousers.

54—55 **I had rather have my horse to my mistress**: a mixture of "I would rather have my horse than my mistress" and "I prefer my horse to my mistress."

56 I would rather my mistress were a jade. (jade: a worthless horse or a loose woman.)

I tell thee, constable, my mistress wears her own hair.

THE CONSTABLE OF FRANCE.

I could make as true a boast as that, if I had a sow to my mistress.

DAUPHIN.

Le chien est retourné à son porpre vomissement, et la truie lavée au bourbier: thou makest use of any thing.

THE CONSTABLE OF FRANCE.

Yet do I not use my horse for my mistress; or any such proverb, so little kin to the purpose.

RAMBURES.

My lord constable, the armor that I saw in your tent to-night,—are those stars or suns upon it?

THE CONSTABLE OF FRANCE.

Stars, my lord.

DAUPHIN.

Some of them will fall to-morrow, I hope.

THE CONSTABLE OF FRANCE.

And yet my sky shall not want.

DAUPHIN.

That may be, for you bear a many superfluously, and 'twere more honor some were away.

THE CONSTABLE OF FRANCE.

Even as your horse bears your praises; who would trot as well, were some of your brags dismounted.

DAUPHIN.

Would I were able to load him with his desert! — Will it never be day? — I will trot to-morrow a mile, and my way shall be paved with English faces.

THE CONSTABLE OF FRANCE.

I will not say so, for fear I should be faced out of my way: but I would it were morning; for I would fain be about the ears of the English.

RAMBURES.

57 wears her own hair: an allusion to the then custom of wearing wigs.

60—61 Le chien… bourbier: “狗所吐的它转过来又吃，猪洗净又回到泥里去滚”(见《圣经·新约·彼得后书》第 2 章 22 节)。

62 for: as.

63 kin: relevant.

70 ’twere more honor some were away: it would be more proper if some (stars) were taken away.

72 dismounted: cut down a peg.

73 Would I were able: I wish I would be able. **load him with his desert**: praise it in terms conmensurate with its merit.

76—77 faced out of my way: outfaced (bullied out of my way); put to shame.

77—78 be about the ears of the English: to give hell to the English.

Who will go to hazard with me for twenty prisoners?

THE CONSTABLE OF FRANCE.

You must first go yourself to hazard, ere you have them.

DAUPHIN.

'Tis midnight; I'll go arm myself. [*Exit*.

DUKE OF ORLEANS.

The Dauphin longs for morning.

RAMBURES.

He longs to eat the English.

THE CONSTABLE OF FRANCE.

I think he will eat all he kills.

DUKE OF ORLEANS.

By the white hand of my lady, he's a gallant prince.

THE CONSTABLE OF FRANCE.

Swear by her foot, that she may tread out the oath.

DUKE OF ORLEANS.

He is, simply, the most active gentleman of France.

THE CONSTABLE OF FRANCE.

Doing is activity: and he will still be doing.

DUKE OF ORLEANS.

He never did harm, that I heard of.

THE CONSTABLE OF FRANCE.

Nor will do none to-morrow: he will keep that good name still.

DUKE OF ORLEANS.

I know him to be valiant.

THE CONSTABLE OF FRANCE.

I was told that by one that knows him better than you.

DUKE OF ORLEANS.

What's he?

THE CONSTABLE OF FRANCE.

Marry, he told me so himself; and he said he cared not who knew it.

DUKE OF ORLEANS.

79 go to hazard：play dice（掷骰子），wager（打赌）。 **for twenty prisoners**：with twenty prisoners as stake.

80 go yourself to hazard：run extreme risks yourself. **ere**：before.

88 Doing is activity：that is，playing the fool is（also）activity. **still be doing**：always be doing it.

91 still：always.

93 I was told that：I was told of that.

95 What's he?：Who is he?

97 knew：should know.

He needs not; it is no hidden virtue in him.

THE CONSTABLE OF FRANCE.

By my faith, sir, but it is; never any body saw it but his lackey: 'tis a hooded valor; and when it appears, it will bate.

DUKE OF ORLEANS.

Ill-will never said well.

THE CONSTABLE OF FRANCE.

I will cap that proverb with — There is flattery in friendship.

DUKE OF ORLEANS.

And I will take up that with — Give the devil his due.

THE CONSTABLE OF FRANCE.

Well placed: there stands your friend for the devil: have at the very eye of that proverb, with — A pox of the devil.

DUKE OF ORLEANS.

You are the better by proverbs, by how much — A fool's bolt is soon shot.

THE CONSTABLE OF FRANCE.

You have shot over.

DUKE OF ORLEANS.

'Tis not the first time you were overshot.

Enter a MESSENGER.

MESSENGER.

My lord high-Constable, the English lie within fifteen hundred paces of your tents.

THE CONSTABLE OF FRANCE.

Who hath measured the ground?

MESSENGER.

The Lord Grandpré.

THE CONSTABLE OF FRANCE.

A valiant and most expert gentleman. — Would it were day! — Alas, poor Harry of England! he longs not

99—100 never … lackey: i.e. only his servant saw his valor (was beaten by him).

100—101 'tis a hooded valor … bate: his valor is hidden most of the time (as a not sufficiently trained falcon is hooded), but when it appears, it will soon abate (as the unhooded falcon will bate, i.e., flap its wings).

103 cap: top, complete.

106 well placed: well said.

106—107 have at the very eye of that proverb: let's have a shot at the bull's eye of that proverb.二人竞相用谚语来抬杠。

107 Pox: a disease such as smallpox or syphilis. **of**: on.

109—110 A fool's bolt (bolt: a blunt-headed arrow) is soon shot: (a proverb) A fool is eager to show off the trick he is up to.

111 shot over: overshot the mark.

112 overshot: beaten in shooting; worsted.

for the dawning, as we do.

DUKE OF ORLEANS.

What a wretched and peevish fellow is this King of England, to mope with his fat-brain'd followers so far out of his knowledge!

THE CONSTABLE OF FRANCE.

If the English had any apprehension, they would run away.

DUKE OF ORLEANS.

That they lack; for if their heads had any intellectual armor, they could never wear such heavy head-pieces.

RAMBURES.

That island of England breeds very valiant creatures; their mastiffs are of unmatchable courage.

DUKE OF ORLEANS.

Foolish curs, that run winking into the mouth of a Russian bear, and have their heads crusht like rotten apples! You may as well say, that's a valiant flea that dare eat his breakfast on the lip of a lion.

THE CONSTABLE OF FRANCE.

Just, just; and the men do sympathize with the mastiffs in robustious and rough coming-on, leaving their wits with their wives: and then give them great meals of beef, and iron and steel, they will eat like wolves, and fight like devils.

DUKE OF ORLEANS.

Ay, but these English are shrewdly out of beef.

THE CONSTABLE OF FRANCE.

Then shall we find to-morrow they have only stomachs to eat, and none to fight. Now is it time to arm; come, shall we about it?

DUKE OF ORLEANS.

It is now two o'clock: but, let me see, — by ten
We shall have each a hundred Englishmen. [*Exeunt*.

120 peevish: silly; thoughtless.

121 mope: move unconsciously. **fat-brain'd**: dull, fat-headed.

121—123 so far out of his knowledge: so as to forget himself.

123 apprehension: perception or sense of fear.

125—126 intellectual armor: brain.

128 mastiffs: English dogs used in bear-baiting.

129 winking: with eyes shut.

133 Just: right; just so. **sympathize**: agree; be in accord.

134 robustious: violent.

138 shrewdly: badly; grievously.

ACT IV PROLOGUE

Enter CHORUS.

CHORUS.

Now entertain conjecture of a tiem
When creeping murmur and the poring dark
Fills the wide vessel of the universe.
From camp to camp, through the foul womb of night,
The hum of either army stilly sounds,
That the fixt sentinels almost receive
The secret whispers of each other's watch:
Fire answers fire; and through their paly flames
Each battle sees the other's umber'd face:
Steed threatens steed, in high and boastful neighs
Piercing the night's dull ear; and from the tents,
The armorers, accomplishing the knights,
With busy hammers closing rivets up,
Give dreadful note of preparation:
The country cocks do crow, the clocks do toll,
And the third hour of drowsy morning name.
Proud of their numbers, and secure in soul,
The confident and over-lusty French
Do the low-rated English play at dice;
And chide the cripple tardy-gaited night,
Who,like a foul and ugly witch, doth limp
So tediously away. The poor condemned English,
Like sacrifices, by their watchful fires
Sit patiently, and inly ruminate
The morning's danger; and their gesture sad
Investing lank-lean cheeks, and war-worn coats,
Presenteth them unto the gazing moon
So many horrid ghosts. O, now, who will behold

IV. Prologue 第四幕开场白。

1 entertain conjecture of：imagine.

2 poring：peering (straining to see), 'poring dark' means it's so dark that a man has to strain his eyes and yet sees little. A case of an epithet being transposed from the person to the thing.

5 stilly：softly.

6 That：so that. **receive**：hear.

8 paly：palish.

9 battle：army. **umber'd**：dark colored (by firelight).

12 accomplishing：finishing the armor of.

13 closing rivets up：nailing down rivets.

14 note：noise.

16 name：(do) strike.

17 secure in soul：overconfident.

18 over-lusty：too merry.

19 low-rated：despised. **play**：play for (with the despised English as stakes).

20 tardy-gaited：slow-moving

21 Who：将 night 拟人化。

24 inly：inwardly. **ruminate**：muse over.

25 gesture sad：serious mien.

26 Investing：accompanying.

The royal captain of this ruin'd band
Walking from watch to watch, from tent to tent,
Let him cry, 'Praise and glory on his head!'
For forth he goes and visits all his host;
Bids them good morrow with a modest smile,
And calls them brothers, friends, and countrymen
Upon his royal face there is no note
How dread an army hath enrounded him;
Nor doth he dedicate one jot of color
Unto the weary and all-watched night;
But freshly looks, and over-bears attaint
With cheerful semblance and sweet majesty;
That every wretch, pining and pale before,
Beholding him, plucks comfort from his looks:
A largess universal, like the sun,
His liberal eye doth give to every one,
Thawing cold fear. Then, mean and gentle all,
Behold, as may unworthiness define,
A little touch of Harry in the night:
And so our scene must to the battle fly;
Where — O for pity! — we shall much disgrace
With four or five most vile and ragged foils,
Right ill-disposed, in brawl ridiculous,
The name of Agincourt. Yet, sit and see;
Minding true things by what their mockeries be.

[*Exit*.

29 **royal captain**：Henry V.

31 **Let him**：接 28 行的 who；等于说 let him who will behold… cry…

35 **note**：sign；indication.

36 **dread**：dreadful. **enrounded**：surrounded.

37—38 **dedicate one…night**：lose any of his rosy color on account of the wearying and wakeful night.

39 **overbears attaint**：overcomes all stain (or infecting influence).

43 **largess**：generosity.

44 **liberal**：bountiful.

45 此处 **Then** 为异读，Q_1 为 that. **mean and gentle all**：all，both people of low rank and gentlefolk.

46 **as may unworthiness define**：as far as my unworthy pen can describe it.

47 **touch**：sketch.

49 **disgrace**：宾语为 name.

50 **foils**：swordsmen.

51 **Right**：entirely. **ill-disposed**：badly managed. **brawl**：squabble.

53 **Minding**：calling to mind. **mockeries**：poor imitations.

SCENE I

The English camp at Agincourt.

Enter KING HENRY, BEDFORD, *and* GLOSTER.

KING HENRY.

Gloster, 'tis true that we are in great danger;
The greater therefore should our courage be.—
Good morrow, brother Bedford.—God Almighty!
There is some soul of goodness in things evil,
Would men observingly distil it out;
For our bad neighbor makes us early stirrers,
Which is both healthful and good husbandry:
Besides, they are our outward consciences,
And preachers to us all; admonishing
That we should dress us fairly for our end.
Thus may we gather honey from the weed,
And make a moral of the devil himself.

Enter ERPINGHAM.

Good morrow, old Sir Thomas Erpingham:
A good soft pillow for that good white head
Were better than a churlish turf of France.

SIR THOMAS ERPINGHAM.

Not so, my liege: this lodging likes me better,
Since I may say, 'Now lie I like a king.'

KING HENRY.

'Tis good for men to love their present pains
Upon example; so the spirit is eased:
And when the mind is quicken'd, out of doubt
The organs, though defunct and dead before,
Break up their drowsy grave, and newly move
With casted slough and fresh legerity.
Lend me thy cloak, Sir Thomas.—Brothers both,

IV.i

4 **soul**：core.

6 **early stirrers**：early risers.

7 **good husbandry**：economy；thrift.

8 **they**：our bad neighbor(s).

10 **dress us**：prepare ourselves. **fairly**：as we should.

12 **make a moral of**(out of)：find a moral lesson in.

15 **churlish**：rough.

16 **likes me**：pleases me.

19 **Upon**：because of.

20 **quicken'd**：stimulated；inspired. **out of doubt**：without doubt.

21 **defunct**：useless；no longer functioning.

23 **casted slough**：cast-off skin (as a snake sheds its skin when it emerges from its hibernation). **legerity**：nimbleness.

24 **Brothers both**：Bedford and Gloster were both Henry V's brothers.

Commend me to the princes in our camp;
Do my good morrow to them; and anon
Desire them all to my pavilion.

DUKE OF GLOSTER.

We shall, my liege.

SIR THOMAS ERPINGHAM.

Shall I attend your Grace?

KING HENRY.

No, my good knight;
Go with my brothers to my lords of England:
I and my bosom must debate awhile,
And then I would no other company.

SIR THOMAS ERPINGHAM.

The Lord in heaven bless thee, noble Harry!

[*Exeunt* GLOSTER, BEDFORD, *and* ERPINGHAM.

KING HENRY.

God-a-mercy, old heart! thou speak'st cheerfully.

Enter PISTOL.

PISTOL.

Qui va là?

KING HENRY.

A friend.

PISTOL.

Discuss unto me; art thou officer?
Or art thou base, common, and popular?

KING HENRY.

I am a gentleman of a company.

PISTOL.

Trail'st thou the puissant pike?

KING HENRY.

Even so. What are you?

PISTOL.

As good a gentleman as the emperor.

KING HENRY.

26 **Do**: give. **good morrow**: good mornig; greetings. **anon**: soon; presently.

27 **to**: to come to.

29 **attend**: accompany.

31 **bosom**: secret thoughts.

34 **God-a-mercy**: (a corruption of "God have mercy") thank you.

35 **Qui va là**: (French) who goes there.

37 **Discuss**: declare.

38 **popular**: plebeian; vulgar.

39 **gentleman of a company**: officer of a company of soldiers.

40 **puissant**: (French) powerful; strong. **The pike**: (镖枪) is grasped in the right hand just below the head, while the staff trails on the ground behind. The question means, "Are you a member of the infantry?"

Then you are a better than the king.

PISTOL.

The king's a bawcock, and a heart of gold,
A lad of life, an imp of fame;
Of parents good, of fist most valiant:
I kiss his dirty shoe, and from heart-string
I love the lovely bully.—What is thy name?

KING HENRY.

Harry *le Roy*.

PISTOL.

Le Roy!
A Cornish name: art thou of Cornish crew?

KING HENRY.

No, I am a Welshman.

PISTOL.

Know'st thou Fluellen?

KING HENRY.

Yes.

PISTOL.

Tell him, I'll knock his leek about his pate
Upon Saint Davy's day.

KING HENRY.

Do not you wear your dagger in your cap that day, lest he knock that about yours.

PISTOL.

Art thou his friend?

KING HENRY.

And his kinsman too.

PISTOL.

The figo for thee, then!

KING HENRY.

I thank you: God be with you!

PISTOL.

My name is Pistol call'd.

[*Exit*.

45 of life: who has seen much life. **imp**: youth.

47 from heart-string: (jocularly) from my heart.

48 bully: fine fellow.

49 le Roy: (from French "le roi") the king.

51 Cornish: 英格兰最西南端 Cornwall 康沃尔郡的。 **crew**: gang.

55 pate: head.

56 Saint Davy's day: Saint David's day — March 1, anniversary of the victory of the Welsh over the Saxons.据说作战时威尔士人帽子上别一棵葱以为标志。见下 IV vii 89.

58 yours: your pate.

61 figo: fig (a derisive term). 见前 III vi 51.

KING HENRY.

It sorts well with your fierceness.

Enter FLUELLEN *and* GOWER, *severally*.

GOWER.

Captain Fluellen!

FLUELLEN.

So! in the name of Cheshu Christ, speak lower. It is the greatest admiration in the universal 'orld, when the true and auncient prerogatifs and laws of the wars is not kept: if you would take the pains but to examine the wars of Pompey the Great, you shall find, I warrant you, that there is no tiddle-taddle nor pribble-pabble in Pompey's camp; I warrant you, you shall find the ceremonies of the wars, and the cares of it, and the forms of it, and the sobriety of it, and the modesty of it, to be otherwise.

GOWER.

Why, the enemy is loud; you heard him all night.

FLUELLEN.

If the enemy is an ass, and a fool, and a prating coxcomb, is it meet, think you, that we should also, look you, be an ass, and a fool, and a prating coxcomb, — in your own conscience, now?

GOWER.

I will speak lower.

FLUELLEN.

I pray you, and peseech you, that you will.

[*Exeunt* GOWER *and* FLUELLEN.

KING HENRY.

Though it appear a little out of fashion,
There is much care and valor in this Welshman.

Enter three SOLDIERS, JOHN BATES, ALEXANDER COURT, *and* MICHAEL WILLIAMS.

ALEXANDER COURT.

Brother John Bates, is not that the morning which

64 **sorts**: agrees.

66 **Cheshu**: Jesus.

67 **admiration**: marvel; wonder.

68 **auncient prerogatifs**(ancient prerogatives): old precedents.

70 **Pompey**: a great Roman general (106—48 B.C.)

71 **no tiddle-taddly nor pibble-pabble**: no babble.

73 **cares**: things to be done; points of attention.

74 **modesty**: moderation

76 **prating coxcomb**: talkative fool.职业的弄臣头戴鸡冠帽,故名coxcomb.

77 **meet**: right; proper.

81 **peseech**: beseech.

82 **out of fashion**: eccentric.

breaks yonder?

JOHN BATES.

I think it be: but we have no great cause to desire the approach of day.

MICHAEL WILLIAMS.

We see yonder the beginning of the day, but I think we shall never see the end of it. — Who goes there?

KING HENRY.

A friend.

MICHAEL WILLIAMS.

Under what captain serve you?

KING HENRY.

Under Sir Thomas Erpingham.

MICHAEL WILLIAMS.

A good old commander and a most kind gentleman: I pray you, what thinks he of our estate?

KING HENRY.

Even as men wrackt upon a sand, that look to be washt off the next tide.

JOHN BATES.

He hath not told his thought to the king?

KING HENRY.

No; nor it is meet he should. For, though I speak it to you, I think the king is but a man, as I am: the violet smells to him as it doth to me; the element shows to him as it doth to me; all his senses have but human conditions: his ceremonies laid by, in his nakedness he appears but a man; and though his affections are higher mounted than ours, yet, when they stoop, they stoop with the like wing. Therefore when he sees reason of fears, as we do, his fears, out of doubt, be of the same relish as ours are: yet, in reason, no man should possess him with any appearance of fear, lest he, by showing it, should dishearten his army.

86 **be**: is.

94 **estate**: condition; state.

95 **wrackt**: wrecked. **look to be**: are likely to be.

98 **meet**: fitting.

100 **element**: sky; heaven. **shows**: looks; appears.

101 **conditions**: qualities.

102 **ceremonies**: trappings.

103—104 **his affections are higher mounted than ours**: his emotions (or feelings) move on a higher plane than ours.

104 **stoop**: swoop down (as a hawk). **like**: similar.

106 **out of doubt**: undoubtedly. **be**: are. **relish**: kind; quality.

107—108 **possess…fear**: put him in possession of (detect in him) any sign of fear.

JOHN BATES.

He may show what outward courage he will; but I believe, as cold a night as 'tis, he could wish himself in Thames up to the neck; — and so I would he were, and I by him, at all adventures, so we were quit here.

KING HENRY.

By my troth, I will speak my conscience of the king: I think he would not wish himself any where but where he is.

JOHN BATES.

Then I would he were here alone; so should he be sure to be ransom'd, and a many poor men's lives saved.

KING HENRY.

I dare say you love him not so ill, to wish him here alone, howsoever you speak this, to feel other men's minds: methinks I could not die any where so contented as in the king's company, — his cause being just, and his quarrel honorable.

MICHAEL WILLIAMS.

That's more than we know.

JOHN BATES.

Ay, or more than we should seek after; for we know enough, if we know we are the king's subjects: if his cause be wrong, our obedience to the king wipes the crime of it out of us.

MICHAEL WILLIAMS.

But if the cause be not good, the king himself hath a heavy reckoning to make, when all those legs and arms and heads, chopt off in battle, shall join together at the latter day, and cry all, 'We died at such a place;' some swearing; some crying for a surgeon; some, upon their wives left poor behind them; some, upon the debts they owe; some, upon their children rawly left. I am afeard there are few die well that die in basttle, for how can they

111 **as**：be it as.

113 **quit here**：finished with this business (war).

114 **conscience**：opinion.

118 **a**：① used for the purpose of indicating that the following objects are regarded collectively as one；② "many" being an old noun，"a many"＝"a many of"，参看 IV iii 95.

120 **to feel**：to test；to sound.

131—132 **the latter day**：the Day of Judgment，世界末日，最后审判日。

135 **rawly**：without due preparation or provision. **afeard**：afraid.

136 **die well**：who die a Christian death.

charitable dispose of any thing, when blood is their argument? Now, if these men do not die well, it will be a black matter for the king that led them to it; who to disobey were against all proportion of subjection.

KING HENRY.

So, if a son, that is by his father sent about merchandise, do sinfully miscarry upon the sea, the imputation of his wickedness, by your rule, should be imposed upon his father that sent him: or if a servant, under his master's command transporting a sum of money, be assail'd by robbers, and die in many irreconciled iniquities, you may call the business of the master the author of the servant's damnation: — but this is not so: the king is not bound to answer the particular endings of his soldiers, the father of his son, nor the master of his servant, for they purpose not their death, when they purpose their services. Besides, there is no king, be his cause never so spotless, if it come to the arbitrement of swords, can try it out with all unspotted soldiers: some peradventure have on them the guilt of premeditated and contrived murder; some, of beguiling virgins with the broken seals of perjury; some, making the wars their bulwark, that have before gored the gentle bosom of peace with pillage and robbery. Now, if these men have defeated the law and outrun native punishment, though they can outstrip men, they have no wings to fly from God: war is His beadle, war is His vengeance; so that here men are punisht for before-breach of the king's laws in now the king's quarrel: where they fear'd the death, they have borne life away; and where they would be safe, they perish: then if they die unprovided, no more is the king guilty of their damnation, than he was befor guilty of those impieties for the which they are now visited. Every subject's duty is the king's; but every subject's soul is

137 charitably dispose of any thing: settle anything in a spirit of charity.

137—138 when blood is their argument: when life or death is the question at issue.

140 proportion of subjection: proper behavior of subjects to their king.

142 do sinfully…sea: is lost at sea without an opportunity to confess his sins.

146 irreconciled iniquities: unconfessed (and unforgiven) sins.

149 bound to answer: responsible for.

151 purpose (*v.t.*): design; intend.

153 arbitrement of swords: decision by swords; battle.

154 unspotted: sinless.

155 contrived: plotted.

156 beguiling: cheating.

156—157 broken seals of perjury: false vows.

157 bulwark: shield.

160 native punishment: punishment in their own country.

162 His: God's. **beadle**: official who handles the arrest and sentencing of lawbreakers, therefore, chastiser.

163 before-breach: previous infringement.

164—165 Where they fear'd…life away: they fled the place where they feared for their life.

165—166 and where they…perish: and they perish at the place where they thought they would be safe.

166 unprovided: without absolution.

168 visited: punished.

his own. Therefore should every soldier in the wars do as every sick man in his bed, — wash every mote out of his conscience: and dying so, death is to him advantage; or not dying, the time was blessedly lost wherein such preparation was gain'd: and in him that escapes, it were not sin to think that, making God so free an offer, He let him outlive that day to see His greatness, and to teach others how they should prepare.

MICHAEL WILLIAMS.

'Tis certain, every man that dies ill, the ill upon his own head, — the king is not to answer it.

JOHN BATES.

I do not desire he should answer for me; and yet I determine to fight lustily for him.

KING HENRY.

I myself heard the king say he would not be ransom'd.

MICHAEL WILLIAMS.

Ay, he said so, to make us fight cheerfully: but when our throats are cut, he may be ransom'd, and we ne'er the wiser.

KING HENRY.

If I live to see it, I will never trust his word after.

MICHAEL WILLIAMS.

'Mass, you'll pay him then! That's a perilous shot out of an elder-gun, that a poor and a private displeasure can do against a monarch! you may as well go about to turn the sun to ice with fanning in his face with a peacock's feather. You'll never trust his word after! come, 'tis a foolish saying.

KING HENRY.

Your reproof is something too round: I should be angry with you, if the time were convenient.

MICHAEL WILLIAMS.

Let it be a quarrel between us, if you live.

171 **mote**：spot；blemish.

175 **so free an offer**：such a free-will offering.

176 **He**：God.

178 **every**：之前省略 as for. **the ill**：后省略 is 或 lies.

179 **answer it**：answer for it.

181 **lustily**：vigorously.

183 **to make**：in order to make.

184 **be ransom'd**：中世纪战争中，被俘的贵族均可赎回，丧身的多为贫困的平民。

187 **'Mass**：by the mass，an oath（protesting the truth of what is said）. **pay**：punish.

188 **elder-gun**：popgun made of elder wood；木雕的儿童玩具枪。**a poor and private**：a poor commoner's.

189 **go about**：undertake.

190 **his**：its，the sun's.

193 **something too round**：somewhat too outspoken（direct）.

195 **quarrel**：dispute. **live**：survive（the war）.

KING HENRY.

I embrace it.

MICHAEL WILLIAMS.

How shall I know thee again?

KING HENRY.

Give me any gage of thine, and I will wear it in my bonnet: then, if ever thou darest acknowledge it, I will make it my quarrel.

MICHAEL WILLIAMS.

Here's my glove: give me another of thine.

KING HENRY.

There.

MICHAEL WILLIAMS.

This will I also wear in my cap: if ever thou come to me and say, after to-morrow, 'This is my glove,' by this hand, I will take thee a box on the ear.

KING HENRY.

If ever I live to see it, I will challenge it.

MICHAEL WILLIAMS.

Thou darest as well be hang'd.

KING HENRY.

Well, I will do it, though I take thee in the king's company.

MICHAEL WILLIAMS.

Keep thy word: fare thee well.

JOHN BATES.

Be friends, you English fools, be friends: we have French quarrels enow, if you could tell how to reckon.

KING HENRY.

Indeed, the French may lay twenty Frenchy crowns to one, they will beat us; for they bear them on their shoulders: but it is no English treason to cut French crowns; and to-morrow the king himself will be a clipper.

[*Exeunt* SOLDIERS.

196 embrace: accept readily (your proposal).

198 gage: token.

201 another: a glove.

205 take thee: give you.

212 enow: enough. **reckon**: settle; cope with.

213—214 lay twenty…to one: 以 20 对 1 打赌。 **crowns**: a pun on the double meaning of the word — "coin" and "head".

214 them: heads (crowns).

215—216 cut…crowns: ① cut heads; ② chip coins.

216 clipper: one who mutilates coins (crowns) by chipping gold from them.

Upon the king! —let us our lives, our souls,
Our debts, our careful wives,
Our children, and our sins, lay on the king!
We must bear all. O hard condition,
Twin-born with greatness, subject to the breath
Of every fool, whose sense no more can feel
But his own wringing!
What infinite heart's-ease must kings neglect,
That private men enjoy!
And what have kings, that privates have not too,
Save ceremony, — save general ceremony?
And what art thou, thou idol ceremony?
What kind of god art thou, that suffer'st more
Of mortal griefs than do thy worshippers?
What are thy rents? what are thy comings-in?
O ceremony, show me but thy worth!
What is thy soul, O adoration?
Art thou aught else but place, degree, and form,
Creating awe and fear in other men?
Wherein thou art less happy being fear'd
Than they in fearing.
What drink'st thou oft, instead of homage sweet,
But poison'd flattery? O, be sick, great greatness,
And bid thy ceremony give thee cure!
Think'st thou the fiery fever will go out
With titles blown from adulation?
Will it give place to flexure and low bending?
Canst thou, when thou command'st the beggar's knee,
Command the health of it? No, thou proud dream,
That play'st so subtly with a king's repose:
I am a king that find thee; and I know
'Tis not the balm, the scepter, and the ball,
The sword, the mace, the crown imperial,
The intertissued robe of gold and pearl.

218 **careful**: full of cares: anxious.

220 **We**: I (royal plural).

221 **Twin-born**: that comes together. **subject to the breath**: exposed to the utterance (comment).

223 **But**: than. **wringing**: torture; suffering.

224 **heart's-ease**: peace of mind. **neglect**: forgo.

225 **private men**: commoners.

227 **Save**: except. **ceremony**: pomp; show of power. **general**: public.

230 **Of**: from.

231 **comings-in**: income.

233 **What…adoration**: what is the essential thing in you that men adore? 此行在 Q_1 为 What is thy soul of adoration? =What is the soul of thy adoration? i.e. What is the essence (secret) of the adoration paid to you?

234 **place, degree, and form**: position, title, and appearance.

236 **Wherein**: in which.

238 **sweet**: gracious.

239 **But**: except.

241—242 Do you think that titles (breaths) blown by adulation can extinguish your fever (sickness) (as if it were a candle flame)

243 **it**: the fever. **give place**: yield. **flexure**: bowing; curtsying. **low bending**: bowing.

244 **command'st … the beggar's knee**: make one who begs a favor of you to kneel.

245 **Command the health of it**: make him give you his health.

247 **find thee**: discover the true character of "dream", i.e. "ceremony".

248 **balm**: oil with which a king is anointed at coronation. **ball**: the golden orb borne together with the scepter as an emblem of sovereignty.

250 **intertissued**: interwoven.

The farced title running 'fore the king,
The throne he sits on, nor the tide of pomp
That beats upon the high shore of this world,—
No, not all these, thrice-gorgeous ceremony,
Not all these, laid in bed majestical,
Can sleep so soundly as the wretched slave,
Who, with a body fill'd and vacant mind,
Gets him to rest, cramm'd with distressful bread;
Never sees horrid night, the child of hell;
But, like a lackey, from the rise to set,
Sweats in the eye of Phœbus, and all night
Sleeps in Elysium; next day, after dawn,
Doth rise, and help Hyperion to his horse;
And follows so the ever-running year,
With profitable labor, to his grave:
And, but for ceremony, such a wretch,
Winding up days with toil and nights with sleep,
Had the fore-hand and vantage of a king.
The slave, a member of the country's peace,
Enjoys it; but in gross brain little wots
What watch the king keeps to maintain the peace,
Whose hours the peasant best advantages.

Enter ERPINGHAM

SIR THOMAS ERPINGHAM.

My lord, your nobles, jealous of your absence,
Seek through your camp to find you.

KING HENRY.

Good old knight,
Collect them all together at my tent:
I'll be before thee.

SIR THOMAS ERPINGHAM.

I shall do 't, my lord. [*Exit*.

KING HENRY.

O God of battles! steel my soldiers' hearts;

251 **The farced … king**: the puffed-up, pompous titles preceding the name of the king, such as "His Most Gracious Majesty," etc.

255 **bed majestical**: a royal bed.

258 **Gets him to rest**: goes to sleep (him—an expletive). **distressful**: earned with distress (by hard work).

259 **sees horrid night**: has a nightmare.

260 **lackey**: running footman. **rise to set**: sun-rise to sun-set.

261 **Phœbus**: 希腊神话中的太阳神。 **the eye of Phœbus**: the sun.

262 **Elysium**: 希腊神话中的天堂。

263 **Hyperion**: 希腊神话中早期巨人 Titans 之一,也是代表太阳之神。

264 **so**: in this manner.

266 **but for**: without.

267 **Winding up**: passing.

268 **Had**: would have. **for-hand**: upper hand; advantage.

270 **it**: peace. **wots**: knows.

272 **advantages**: takes advantage of.

273 **jealous of**: disturbed by.

276 **shall**: will.

Possess them not with fear; take from them now
The sense of reckoning, if th' opposed numbers
Pluck their hearts from them! —Not to-day, O Lord,
O, not to-day, think not upon the fault
My father made in compassing the crown!
I Richard's body have interred new;
And on it have bestow'd more contrite tears
Than from it issued forced drops of blood:
Five hundred poor I have in yearly pay,
Who twice a-day their wither'd hands hold up
Toward heaven, to pardon blood; and I have built
Two chantries, where the sad and solemn priests
Sing still for Richard's soul. More will I do;
Though all that I can do is nothing worth,
Since that my penitence comes after all,
Imploring pardon.

Enter GLOSTER

DUKE OF GLOSTER.

My liege!

KING HENRY.

My brother Gloster's voice? —Ay;
I know thy errand, I will go with thee:—
The day, my friends, and all things stay for me.

[*Exeunt*.

SCENE II

The French camp.

Enter the DAUPHIN, ORLEANS, RAMBURES, *and others*.

DUKE OF ORLEANS.

The sun doth gild our armor; up, my lords!

DAUPHIN.

Montez à cheval! — My horse! *varlet*, *laquais*! ha!

279 sense of reckoning: ability of counting numbers. **th' opposed numbers**: the forces of the enemy.

281 fault: treason.

282 My father: Henry IV，他是篡位得的王位。 **compassing**: obtaining.

283 Richard: Richard II，他被 Henry IV 篡位后，又被 Henry 指使的人谋杀于 Pomfret. 亨利五世即位后把 Richard 的尸体重葬于威斯敏斯特寺。 **new**: anew.

286 have: employ.

288 pardon blood: ask for pardon for bloodshed.

289 chantries: monasteries. **sad**: serious.

290 still: always; continuously.

292—293 Since, after all, it is not out of benevolence that I do these things, but from my penitence and with the purpose of imploring your (God's) pardon.

296 stay for: wait for.

IV. ii

2 Montez à cheval: Shakespeare's French for 'mount your horse'. It is not idiomatic, for the French would simply say 'à cheval'. **var-let**: valet; attendant. **laquais**: lackey; running footman.

DUKE OF ORLEANS.
O brave spirit!
DAUPHIN.
Via! — *les eaux et la terre*, —
DUKE OF ORLEANS.
Rien puis? l'air et le feu, —
DAUPHIN.
Ciel! cousin Orleans.

Enter CONSTABLE.

Now, my lord Constable!
THE CONSTABLE OF FRANCE.
Hark, how our steeds for present service neigh!
DAUPHIN.
Mount them, and make incision in their hides,
That their hot blood may spin in English eyes,
And dout them with superfluous courage, ha!
RAMBURES.
What, will you have them weep our horses' blood?
How shall we, then, behold their natural tears?

Enter a MESSENGER

MESSENGER.
The English are embattled, you French peers.
THE CONSTABLE OF FRANCE.
To horse, you gallant princes! straight to horse!
Do but behold yond poor and starved band,
And your fair show shall suck away their souls,
Leaving them but the shales and husks of men.
There is not work enough for all our hands;
Scarce blood enough in all their sickly veins
To give each naked curtle-axe a stain,
That our French gallants shall to-day draw out,
And sheathe for lack of sport: let us but blow on them,
The vapor of our valor will o'erturn them.
'Tis positive 'gainst all exceptions, lords,

4 Via! —les eaux et la terre：away，water and earth（上面王子曾夸称他的骏马是纯粹的“风”和“火”，根本没有重浊的“水”和“土”，见 III. vii 18.）

5 Rien puis? l'air et le feu：Nothing more? air and fire.

6 ciel：the sky.

8 present：immediate.

9 make incision in their hides：spur them.

10 That：so that. **spin in**：gush forth into.

11 dout them：put them out；extinguish.

14 embattled：in battle array.

18 shales：shells.

21 curtle-axe：cutlass，弯刀。

23 sport：fighting.

25 'Tis positive 'gainst all exceptions：there is no doubt about that.

That our superfluous lackeys and our peasants,—
Who in unnecessary action swarm
About our squares of battle, —were enow
To purge this field of such a hilding foe;
Though we upon this mountain's basis by
Took stand for idle speculation,—
But that our honor must not. What's to say?
A very little little let us do,
And all is done. Then let the trumpets sound
The tucket-sonance and the note to mount:
For our approach shall so much dare the field,
That England shall couch down in fear, and yield.

Enter GRANDPRÉ

GRANDPRÉ.

Why do you stay so long, my lords of France?
Yond island carrions, desperate of their bones,
Ill-favoredly become the morning field:
Their ragged curtains poorly are let loose,
And our air shakes them passing scornfully:
Big Mars seems bankrout in their beggar'd host,
And faintly through a rusty beaver peeps:
The horsemen sit like fixed candlesticks,
With torch-staves in their hand;and their poor jades
Lob down their heads, dropping the hides and hips,
The gum down-roping from their pale-dead eyes,
And in their pale dull mouths the gimmal-bit
Lies foul with chew'd grass, still and motionless;
And their executors, the knavish crows,
Fly o'er them, all impatient for their hour.
Description cannot suit itself in words
To demonstrate the life of such a battle
In life so lifeless as it shows itself.

THE CONSTABLE OF FRANCE.

They have said their prayers, and they stay for death.

28 squares of battle：squadrons；方阵。

29 hilding：sorry；worthless.

30 basis：foot. **by**：nearby.

31 speculation：looking on.

32 must not：forbids. **What 's to say?**：What is to be said?

35 tucket-sonance(tucket sound)：flourish on a trumpet. **note**：signal.

36 dare：dazzle；daze.据说百灵鸟看到小鹰、镜子或红布就被怔慑，容易捉住。

39 Yond：yonder. **island**：因英国系岛国，此字代英国。**carrions**：行尸走肉的人。 **desperate of their bones**：recklessly risking their bones.

40 ill-favoredly：unpleasingly；badly. **become**：befit；suit.

41 curtains：colors；军旗。

42 passing (*adv.*)：exceedingly.

43 Mars：希腊神话中的战神。 **bankrout**：bankrupt.

44 faintly：timidly. **beaver**：helmet visor.

47 Lob down：hang down；droop. **dropping**：sagging.

48 gum：watery matter secreted by glands. **down-roping**：hanging，参看 III. v 25.

49 gimmal-bit：a bit made of links.

51 their executors：the crows which are to prey on their carcasses.

53 suit itself in words：find suitable words.

DAUPHIN.

Shall we go send them dinners and fresh suits,
And give their fasting horses provender,
And after fight with them?

THE CONSTABLE OF FRANCE.

I stay but for my guidon: — to the field! —
I will the banner from a trumpet take,
And use it for my haste. Come, come, away!
The sun is high, and we outwear the day. [*Exeunt*.

SCENE III

The English camp.

Enter GLOSTER, BEDFORD, EXETER, ERPINGHAM, *with all his host*; SALISBURY, *and* WESTMORELAND.

DUKE OF GLOSTER.

Where is the king?

DUKE OF BEDFORD.

The king himself is rode to view the battle.

EARL OF WESTMORELAND.

Of fighting-men they have full three-score thousand.

DUKE OF EXETER.

There's five to one; besides, they all are fresh.

EARL OF SALISBURY.

God's arm strike with us! 'tis a fearful odds.
God b' wi' you, princes all; I'll to my charge:
If we no more meet till we meet in heaven,
Then, joyfully,—my noble Lord of Bedford,—
My dear Lord Gloster, —and my good Lord Exeter,—
And my kind kinsman, — warriors all, adieu!

DUKE OF BEDFORD.

Farewell, good Salisbury; and good luck go with thee!

DUKE OF EXETER.

59 **after**：afterwards；then.

60 **guidon**：standard；banner. 此行在对折本中作“guide. On to the field!”

61 **trumpet**：①trumpeter；② banner from a trumpet 军号下悬挂的小旗。

62 **for**：because of.

63 **outwear**：are wasting.

IV. iii

2 **is rode**：has ridden.

5 **God's arm strike with us!**：May God's arm strike for us.

6 **God b' wi' you**：God be with you. **charge**：battle station.

10 **my kind kinsman**：referring to Westmoreland, because Westmoreland's younger son was married to Salisbury's daughter.

Farewell, kind lord; fight valiantly to-day:
And yet I do thee wrong to mind thee of it,
For thou art framed of the firm truth of valor.
[*Exit* SALISBURY.

DUKE OF BEDFORD.

He is as full of valor as of kindness;
Princely in both.

Enter KING HENRY

EARL OF WESTMORELAND.

O, that we now had here
But one ten thousand of those men in England
That do no work to-day!

KING HENRY.

What's he that wishes so?
My cousin Westmoreland? — No, my fair cousin:
If we are markt to die, we are enow
To do our country loss; and if to live,
The fewer men, the greater share of honor.
God's will! I pray thee, wish not one man more.
By Jove, I am not covetous for gold;
Nor care I who doth feed upon my cost;
It yearns me not if men my garments wear;
Such outward things dwell not in my desires:
But if it be a sin to covet honor,
I am the most offending soul alive.
No, faith, my coz, wish not a man from England:
God's peace! I would not lose so great an honor,
As one man more, methinks, would share from me,
For the best hope I have. O, do not wish one more!
Rather proclaim it, Westmoreland, through my host,
That he which hath no stomach to this fight,
Let him depart; his passport shall be made,
And crowns for convoy put into his purse:
We would not die in that man's company

13 **mind**: remind.

14 **framed**: built.

16 **O, that we now had here**: how good it would be if we had here now.

17 **But**: only.

18 **What's he**: Who is he.

20 **markt**: marked; destined. **enow**: enough.

23 **God' will**: a mild oath.

24 **By Jove**: an oath. Originally it was probably "By Heaven", and then the 1605 Act against profanity on the stage made the players change it.

25 **feed upon my cast**: live at my expense; live off me.

26 **yearns**: grieves.

27 **outward things**: 身外之物。 **dwell not**: have no place.

29 **offending**: sinful.

30 **coz**: cousin.

32 **methinks**: it seems to me.

33 **For**: in spite of.

34 **through my host**: to my whole army.

35 **which**: who. **to**: for.

37 **crowns**: 一克朗值五先令。 **convoy**: traveling expenses.

That fears his fellowship to die with us.
This day is call'd the feast of Crispian:
He that outlives this day, and comes safe home,
Will stand a tip-toe when this day is named,
And rouse him at the name of Crispian.
He that shall live this day, and see old age,
Will yearly on the vigil feast his neighbors,
And say, 'To-morrow is Saint Crispian:'
Then will he strip his sleeve and show his scars,
And say, 'These wounds I had on Crispin's day.'
Old men forget; yet all shall be forgot,
But he'll remember with advantages
What feats he did that day: then shall our names,
Familiar in their mouths as household words,—
Harry the king, Bedford and Exeter,
Warwick and Talbot, Salisbury and Gloster,—
Be in their flowing cups freshly remember'd.
This story shall the good man teach his son;
And Crispin Crispian shall ne'er go by,
From this day to the ending of the world,
But we in it shall be remembered,—
We few, we happy few, we band of brothers;
For he to-day that sheds his blood with me
Shall be my brother; be he ne'er so vile,
This day shall gentle his condition:
And gentlemen in England now a-bed
Shall think themselves accurst they were not here;
And hold their manhoods cheap whiles any speaks
That fought with us upon Saint Crispin's day.

Enter SALISBURY.

EARL OF SALISBURY.

My sovereign lord, bestow yourself with speed:
The French are bravely in their battles set,
And will with all expedience charge on us.

39 That fears…us: who fears to be my companion in death.

40 the feast of Crispian: October 25, a day on which people used to commemorate Crispinus and Crispianus, Roman brothers who went to France to advance Christianity, were thrown into a caldron of boiling lead by Maximianus in 287 A.D. and were honored as martyrs and patron saints of shoemakers.

42 a: on

43 rouse him: feel elated.

44 shall live: should survive.

45 vigil: eve of a festival.

50 But: only. **advantages**: interest; additions and elaborations.

62 ne'er: ever. **vile**: of such humble birth.

63 gentle his condition: advance him to the rank of gentleman.

66 hold their manhoods cheap: despise their manhood.

66—67 whiles any speaks That: when anybody who…speaks.

68 bestow yourself: go to your places,见下第78行。

69 bravely: in gallant array. **battles**: battle arrays.

70 expedience: haste.

KING HENRY.

All things are ready, if our minds be so.

EARL OF WESTMORELAND.

Perish the man whose mind is backward now!

KING HENRY.

Thou dost not wish more help from England, coz?

EARL OF WESTMORELAND.

God's will! my liege, would you and I alone,
Without more help, might fight this battle out!

KING HENRY.

Why, now thou hast unwisht five thousand men;
Which likes me better than to wish us one.—
You know your places: God be with you all!

Tucket. Enter MONTJOY.

MONTJOY.

Once more I come to know of thee, King Harry,
If for thy ransom thou wilt now compound,
Before thy most assured overthrow:
For certainly thou art so near the gulf,
Thou needs must be englutted. Besides, in mercy,
The Constable desires thee thou wilt mind
Thy followers of repentance; that their souls
May make a peaceful and a sweet retire
From off these fields, where, wretches, their poor bodies
Must lie and fester.

KING HENRY.

Who hath sent thee now?

MONTJOY.

The Constable of France.

KING HENRY.

I pray thee, bear my former answer back:
Bid them achieve me, and then sell my bones.
Good God! why should they mock poor fellows thus?

72 **Perish the man**：let that man die.

76 **unwisht**：wished away. 据霍林谢德史书，当时英军有步骑兵共一万五千人。

77 **likes me better**：pleases me more. **that to wish us one**：than to wish that we should have one more fighter.

79 **of**：from.

80 **compound**：settle the quarrel.

82 **gulf**：whirlpool.

83 **englutted**：swallowed up.

84 **desires thee thou**：desires that you. **wilt mind**：would remind.

86 **retire**：retreat.

88 **fester**：rot.

91 **achieve me**：bring me to my end；slay me.

The man that once did sell the lion's skin
While the beast lived, was kill'd with hunting him.
A many of our bodies shall no doubt
Find native graves; upon the which, I trust,
Shall witness live in brass of this day's work:
And those that leave their valiant bones in France,
Dying like men, though burieed in your dunghills,
They shall be famed; for there the sun shall greet them,
And draw their honors reeking up to heaven;
Leaving their earthly parts to choke your clime,
The smell whereof shall breed a plague in France.
Mark, then, abounding valor in our English;
That, being dead, like to the bullet's grazing,
Break out into a second course of mischief,
Killing in relapse of mortality.
Let me speak proudly: —tell the Constable
We are but warriors for the working-day;
Our gayness and our gilt are all besmircht
With rainy marching in the painful field;
There's not a piece of feather in our host,—
Good argument, I hope, we will not fly,—
And time hath worn us into slovenry:
But, by the mass, our hearts are in the trim;
And my poor soldiers tell me, yet ere night
They 'll be in fresher robes; or they will pluck
The gay new coats o'er the French soldier's heads,
And turn them out of service. If they do this,—
As, if God please, they shall,—my ransom then
Will soon be levied. Herald, save thou thy labor;
Come thou no more for ransom, gentle herald:
They shall have none, I swear, but these my joints,—
Which if they have as I will leave 'em them,
Shall yield them little, tell the Constable.

MONTJOY.

94 **with**: while. **him**: it.

95 **A many**: a great number. 参看 IV. i 115.

96 **native**: English. **the which**: their graves.

97 **brass**: (used to symbolize imperishableness) epitaphs made of brass. 英名人墓上常有铜像或铜碑记载功勋。

99 **dunghills**: 对法国山河的鄙称。

102 **earthly parts**: corpses. **choke**: contaminate; poison.

103 **whereof**: of which.

104 **abounding**: abundant.

105 **grazing**: ricocheting; rebounding.

107 **relapse**: ① falling back into their elements; decomposition; ② rebound.

109 **for the working day**: in working clothes, not here on holiday.

110 **Our gayness and our gilt**: our splendid trappings.

111 **painful**: laborious; toilsome.

113 **argument**: proof; evidence. **will not fly**: have no intention of flying.

114 **slovenry**: slovenliness.

115 **by the mass**: an oath (protesting the truth of what is said). **in the trim**: in fine condition.

116 **yet**: however.

119 **turn them out of service**: disarm them (the French soldiers).

120 **shall**: are destined to do.

121 **levied**: collected.

122 **gentle**: honorable, a complimentary epithet.

123 **but**: except. **joints**: hones.

I shall, King harry. And so, fare thee well:
Thou never shalt hear herald any more. [*Exit*.

KING HENRY.

I fear thou 'lt once more come again for ransom.

Enter YORK.

DUKE OF YORK.

My lord, most humbly on my knee I beg
The leading of the vaward.

KING HENRY.

Take it, brave York. — Now, soldiers, march away: —
And how thou pleasest, God, dispose the day! [*Exeunt*.A

SCENE IV

The field of battle.

Alarum: *excursions*. *Enter* PISTOL, *French* SOLDIER, *and* BOY.

PISTOL.

Yield, cur!

FRENCH SOLDIER.

Je pense que vous êtes le gentilhomme de bonne qualité.

PISTOL.

Qualtitie calmie custure me! Art thou a gentleman? what is thy name? discuss.

FRENCH SOLDIER.

O Seigneur Dieu!

PISTOL.

O, signieur Dew should be a gentleman:—
Perpend my words, O Signieur Dew, and mark;—
O Signieur Dew, thou diest on point of fox,
Except, O signieur, thou do give to me
Egregious ransom.

FRENCH SOLDIER.

O, *prenez miséricorde*! *ayez pitié de moy*!

130 **vaward**: vanguard.

131 **York**: Edward, Duke of York.

132 **how**: however.

IV. iv

excursions: military sorties.

2 I believe that you are a gentleman of good quality.

3 **Qualtitie calmie custure me!**: Pistol's invented French.

4 **discuss**: declare.

5 **Seigneur Dieu**: Lord God; but Pistol, who knows little French, mistakes this for the soldier's name.

7 **Perpend**: consider; weigh.

8 **fox**: a common word for sword; the figure of a fox was engraved on a certain kind of sword as the trade-mark.

10 **Egregious**: extraordinarily high.

11 Show mercy, take pity on me.

PISTOL.

Moy shall not serve; I will have forty moys;
Or I will fetch thy rim out at thy throat
In drops of crimson blood.

FRENCH SOLDIER.

Est-il impossible d'échapper la force de ton bras?

PISTOL.

Brass, cur!
Thou damned and luxurious mountain-goat,
Offer'st me brass?

FRENCH SOLDIER.

O, pardonnez-moy!

PISTOL.

Say'st thou me so? is that a ton of moys? —
Come hither, boy: ask me this slave in French
What is his name.

BOY.

Ecoutez: comment êtes-vous appelé?

FRENCH SOLDIER.

Monsieur le Fer.

BOY.

He says his name is Master Fer.

PISTOL.

Master Fer! I'll fer him, and firk him, and ferret him: — discuss the same in French unto him.

BOY.

I do not know the French for fer, and ferret, and firk.

PISTOL.

Bid him prepare; for I will cut his throat.

FRENCH SOLDIER.

Que dit-il, monsieur?

BOY.

Il me commande de vous dire que vous faites vous prêt; car ce soldat ici est disposé tout à cette heure de couper

12 **Moy**: Pistol thinks that moy (moi=me) is a coin.

13 **rim**: the lining of one's stomach.

15 Is it impossible to escape the force of your arm?

16 **Brass**: Pistol mistakes the French word 'bras' (=arm) for the English word "brass" (=copper).

17 **luxurious**: lustful.

19 O pardon me!

20 **me**: 前省略 to. **a ton of moys**: Pistol's misconstruction of "pardonnez-moy".

23 Listen: how are you called?

26 **firk**: beat. **ferret**: worry (as a ferret worries a rat before killing it).

30 What did he say, master?

31—33 He commands me to tell you to be prepared (for the worst), for this soldier here is disposed (determined) at this moment to cut your throat.

votre gorge.

PISTOL.

Owy, cuppele gorge, permafoy,
Peasant, unless thou give me crowns, brave crowns;
Or mangled shalt thou be by this my sword.

FRENCH SOLDIER.

O, je vous supplie, pour l'amour de dieu, me pardonner! Je suis gentilhomme de bonne maison: gardez ma vie, et je vous donnerai deux cents écus.

PISTOL.

What are his words?

BOY.

He prays you to save his life: he is a gentleman of a good house; and for his ransom he will give you two hundered crowns.

PISTOL.

Tell him my fury shall abate, and I
The crowns will take.

FRENCH SOLDIER.

Petit monsieur, que dit-il?

BOY.

Encore qu'il est contre son jurement de pardonner aucun prisonnier, néanmoins, pour les écus que vous l'avez promis, il est content de vous donner la liberté, le franchisement.

FRENCH SOLDIER.

Sur mes genoux je vous donne mille remercimens; et je m'estime heureux que je suis tombé entre les mains d'un chevalier, je pense, le plus brave, vaillant, et très distingué seigneur d'Angleterre.

PISTOL.

Expound unto me, boy.

BOY.

He gives you, upon his knees, a thousand thanks; and he esteems himself happy that he hath fallen into the

34 Yes, cut the throat, by my faith.

35 **unless**: either. **brave**: fine.

37—39 O, I beg of you, for the love of God, to pardon me. I am a gentleman of good family: spare my life and I'll give you two hundred écus（法旧币，一 écu 值三法郎）。

46 Young master, what did he say?

47—49 Though it is against his judgment to pardon any prisoner; nevertheless, for the écus you have promised him, he is willing to give you liberty.

50—53 Upon my knees I give you a thousand thanks, and I consider myself happy that I have fallen into the hands of a chevalier who I think is the most brave, valorous and a very distinguished lord of England.

54 **Expound unto me**: explain to me.

hands of one, as he thinks, the most brave, valorous, and thrice-worthy signieur of England.

PISTOL.

As I suck blood, I will some mercy show. — Follow me, cur.

[*Exit*.

BOY.

Suivez-vous le grand capitaine. [*Exit* FRENCH SOLDIER.] I did never know so full a voice issue from so empty a heart: but the saying is true, — The empty vessel makes the greatest sound. Bardolph and Nym had ten times more valor than this roaring devil i'th'old play, that every one may pare his nails with a wooden dagger; and they are both hang'd; and so would this be, if he durst steal any thing adventurously. I must stay with the lackeys, with the luggage of our camp: the French might have a good prey of us, if he knew of it; for there is none to guard it but boys. [*Exit*.

SCENE V

Another part of the field.

Enter CONSTABLE, ORLEANS, BOURBON, DAUPHIN, RAMBURES, *and others*.

THE CONSTABLE OF FRANCE.

O diable!

DUKE OF ORLEANS.

O Seigneur! — *le jour est perdu*, *tout est perdu*!

DAUPHIN.

Mort de ma vie! all is confounded, all!
Reproach and everlasting shame
Sit mocking in our plumes. — *O méchante fortune*! —
Do not run away. [*A short alarum*.

61 Suivez-vous... capitaine: Follow the great captain.

65 roaring devil i' th' old play: in the old miracle plays, the devil usually entered roaring and carrying a wooden dagger or sword.

68 adventurously: boldly.

69—70 have a good prey of us: get a good booty from us.

IV. v

1 O devil!

2 O Lord! the day is lost, all is lost.

3 Mort de ma vie!: Death upon my life, an oath. **confounded**: ruined; lost.

5 méchante fortune!: ill fortune.

6 broke: broken.

THE CONSTABLE OF FRANCE.

Why, all our ranks are broke.

DAUPHIN.

O perdurable shame! — let's stab ourselves.
Be these the wretches that we play'd at dice for?

DUKE OF ORLEANS.

Is this the king we sent to for his ransom?

DUKE OF BOURBON.

Shame, and eternal shame, nothing but shame!
Let's die in honour: once more back again;
And he that will not follow bourbon now,
Let him go hence, and with his cap in hand,
Like a base pandar, hold the chamber-door
Whilst by a slave, no gentler than my dog,
His fairest daughter is contaminate.

THE CONSTABLE OF FRANCE.

Disorder, that hath spoil'd us, friend us now!
Let us on heaps go offer up our lives.

DUKE OF ORLEANS.

We are enow, yet living in the field,
To smother up the English in our throngs,
If any order might be thought upon.

DUKE OF BOURBON.

The devil take order now! I'll to the throng:
Let life be short; else shame will be too long. [*Exeunt*.

SCENE VI

Another part of the field.

Alarum. Enter KING HENRY *and* FORCES, EXETER, *and others.*

KING HENRY.

Well have we done, thrice-valiant countrymen:
But all's not done; yet keep the French the field.

7 **perdurable**: lasting; enduring.

8 **Be**: are.

11 **back**: go back.

14 **pandar**: pander; Pmp (from Pandarus).

15 **gentler**: better born.

15—16 自然顺序为 Whilst his fairest daughter is contaminate by a slave, no…

16 **contaminate**: contaminated; violate.

17 **spoil'd**: ruined. **friend**: befriend.

18 **on heaps**: in a body.

19 **We are…field**: ther are still enough of us living in the field.

21 **thought upon**: contrived; brought about.

IV. vi

2 **yet**: still.

DUKE OF EXETER.

The Duke of York commends him to your majesty.

KING HENRY.

Lives he, good uncle? thrice within this hour
I saw him down; thrice up again, and fighting;
From helmet to the spur all blood he was.

DUKE OF EXETER.

In which array, brave soldier, doth he lie,
Larding the plain; and by his bloody side,
Yoke-fellow to his honor-owing wounds,
The noble Earl of Suffolk also lies.
Suffolk first died: and York, all haggled over,
Comes to him, where in gore he lay insteept,
And takes him by the beard; kisses the gashes
That bloodily did yawn upon his face;
And cries aloud, 'Tarry, dear cousin Suffolk!
My soul shall thine keep company to heaven;
Tarry, sweet soul, for mine, then fly abreast;
As in this glorious and well-foughten field
We kept together in our chivalry!'
Upon these words I came, and cheer'd him up:
He smiled me in the face, raught me his hand,
And, with a feeble gripe, says, 'Dear my lord,
Commend my service to my sovereign.'
So did he turn, and over Suffolk's neck
He threw his wounded arm, and kist his lips;
And so, espoused to death, with blood he seal'd
A testament of noble-ending love.
The pretty and sweet manner of it forced
Those waters from me which I would have stopt;
But I had not so much of man in me,
And all my mother came into mine eyes,
And gave me up to tears.

KING HENRY.

6 **all blood**: covered with blood.

7 **In which array**: in such a state (i. e., covered all over with blood).

8 **Larding**: enriching (with his blood).

9 **Yoke-fellow**: companion. **honor-owing**: honorable.

11 **all haggled over**: hacked (cut) all over his body.

12 **gore**: blood. **insteept**: steeped in; soaked.

15 **Tarry**: wait.

18 **well-foughten**: well-fought.

19 **kept together**: matched each other. **chivalry**: bravery.

21 **smiled me in the face**: smiled into my face. **raught me his hand**: reached for my hand (raught 为 reach 的旧体过去分词形式)。

22 **gripe**: grip.

24 **So**: Then.

26 **espoused**: wedded.

28 **pretty**: lovely.

29 **waters**: tears.

30 **But**: only.

31 **all my mother**: all the feminine softness in me.

I blame you not;
For, hearing this, I must perforce compound
With mistful eyes, or they will issue too. — [*Alarum*.
But, hark! what new alarum is this same? —
The French have reinforced their scatter'd men: —
Then every soldier kill his prisoners;
Give the word through. [*Exeunt*.

SCENE VII

Another part of the field.

Enter FLUELLEN *and* GOWER.

FLUELLEN.

Kill the poys and the luggage! 'tis expressly against the law of arms: 'tis as arrant a piece of knavery, mark you now, as can be offert; in your conscience, now, is it not?

GOWER.

'Tis certain there's not a boy left alive; and the cowardly rascals that ran from the battle ha' done this slaughter: besides, they have burn'd and carried away all that was in the king's tent; wherefore the king, most worthily, hath caused every soldier to cut his prisoner's throat. O, 'tis a gallant king!

FLUELLEN.

Ay, he was porn at Monmouth, Captain Gower. What call you the town's name where Alexander the Pig was porn?

GOWER.

Alexander the Great.

FLUELLEN.

Why, I pray you, is not pig great? the pig, or the great, or the mighty, or the huge, or the magnanimous, are all one reckonings, save the phrase is a little variations.

33 **perforce**：by constraint.

33—34 **compound/With**：come to terms with.

34 **issue**：shed tears.

37 **Then**：后等于省略 see that.

38 Issue the order to all.

IV. vii

1 **Kill the poys and the luggage**：the English equipment was guarded by boys and lackeys，who were attacked by some of the French soldiers and killed，and the luggage plundered.

2 **arrant**：out-and-out.

3 **offert**：offered；committed.

7 **wherefore**：therefore. **worthily**：justifiably.

10 **porn**：born. **Monmouth**：county town of the former county of Monmouthshire in west England，but for most purposes considered part of Wales.

11 **pig**：big.

15—16 **all one reckonings**：of the same value. Fluellen 用字的单复数也不对。

GOWER.

I think Alexander the Great was born in Macedon: his father was call'd Philip of Macedon, as I take it.

FLUELLEN.

I think it is in Macedon where Alexander is porn. I tell you, captain, if you look in the maps of the 'orld, I warrant you sall find, in the comparisons between Macedon and Monmouth, that the situastions, look you, is both alike. There is a river in Macedon; and there is also moreover a river at Monmouth: it is called Wye at Monmouth; but it is out of my prains what is the name of the other river; but 'tis all one, 'tis alike as my fingers is to my fingers, and there is salmons in both. If you mark Alexander's life well, Harry of Monmouth's life is come after it indifferent well; for there is figures in all things. Alexander, — Got knows, and you know, — in his rages, and his furies, and his wraths, and his cholers, and his moods, and his displeasures, and his indignations, and also being a little intoxicates in his prains, did, in his ales and his angers, look you, kill his pest friend, Cleitus.

GOWER.

Our king is not like him in that: he never kill'd any of his friends.

FLUELLEN.

It is not well done, mark you now, to take the tales out of my mouth, ere it is made and finisht. I speak but in the figures and comparisons of it: as Alexander kill'd his friend Cleitus, being in his ales and his cups; so also Harry Monmouth, being in his right wits and his goot judgements, turn'd away the fat knight with the great-pelly doublet: he was full of jests, and gipes, and knaveries, and mocks; I have forgot his name.

GOWER.

Sir John Falstaff.

21 **sall**：shall.

25 **it is out of my prains** (brains)：I have forgotten.

26 **all one**：all the same；no matter.

27 **both**：both rivers.

28 **is come after it**：resembles it.

28—29 **indifferent**：fairly.

29 **figures**：parallels；prototypes.

31 **cholers**：ill humors.

33 **intoxicates**：intoxicated；crazy.

34 **pest**：best. **Cleitus**：是亚历山大大帝从小最好的朋友，在公元前 327 年一次宴席上他批评亚历山大骄傲，被用矛杀死。

37—38 **take the tales out of my mouth**：interrupt my narration.

38 **ere**：before. **finisht**：finished.

42—43 **the fat knight … doublet**：Falstaff (the lower part of the doublet was sometimes called the 'belly', and this might be 'great' or 'thin')见《亨利四世下篇》。

43 **gipes**：gibes.

FLUELLEN.

That is he: — I'll tell you there is goot men porn at Monmouth.

GOWER.

Here comes his majesty.

Alarum. Enter KING HENRY *and* FORCES; WARWICK, GLOSTER, EXETER, *and others.*

KING HENRY.

I was not angry since I came to France
Until this instant. — Take a trumpet, herald;
Ride thou unto the horsemen on yond hill:
If they will fight with us, bid them come down,
Or void the field; they do offend our sight:
If they 'll do neither, we will come to them,
And make them skirr away, as swift as stones
Enforced from the old Assyrian slings:
Besides, we 'll cut the throats of those we have;
And not a man of them that we shall take
Shall taste our mercy: — go, and tell them so.

DUKE OF EXETER.

Here comes the herald of the French, my liege.

DUKE OF GLOSTER.

His eyes are humbler than they used to be.

Enter MONTJOY.

KING HENRY.

How now! what means this, herald? know'st thou not
That I have fined these bones of mine for ransom?
Comest thou again for ransom?

MONTJOY.

No, great king:
I come to thee for charitable licence
That we may wander o'er this bloody field
To look our dead, and then to bury them;
To sort our nobles from our common men;

49 **I was not angry**：I have never been angry.

51 **yond**：yonder；over there.

53 **void**：quit.

55 **skirr**：scurry.

56 **Enforced**：driven by force. **slings**：捧石器。

63 **fined**：promised to pay as a fine.

65 **licence**：permission.

67 **look**：look for.（有的版本作 book：register）

68 **sort**：separate.

For many of our princes — woe the while —
Lie drown'd and soakt in mercenary blood;
So do our vulgar drench their peasant limbs
In blood of princes; and their wounded steeds
Fret fetlock deep in gore, and with wild rage
Yerk out their armed heels at their dead masters,
Killing them twice. O, give us leave, great king,
To view the field in safety, and dispose
Of their dead bodies!

KING HENRY.

I tell thee truly, herald,
I know not if the day be ours or no;
For yet a many of your horsemen peer
And gallop o'er the field.

MONTJOY.

The day is yours.

KING HENRY.

Praised be God, and not our strength, for it! —
What is this castle call'd that stands hard by?

MONTJOY.

They call it Agincourt.

KING HENRY.

Then call we this the field of Agincourt,
Fought on the day of Crispin Crispianus.

FLUELLEN.

Your grandfather of famous memory, an't please your majesty, and your great-uncle Edward the Plack Prince of Wales, as I have read in the chronichles, fought a most prave pattle here in France.

KING HENRY.

They did, Fluellen.

FLUELLEN.

Your majesty says very true: if your majesties is remember'd of it, the Welshmen did goot service in a garden

69 woe the while：alas.

70 mercenary blood：blood of common soldiers who fought for money.

72 blood：前省略 the.

73 Fret：烦躁不安。 **fetlock deep**：up to their fetlocks（马蹄上部的毛）。 **gore**：blood.

74 Yerk out：Lash out. **armed**：spiked；装有铁刺的。

79 a many of，见 IV. iii 95 注。 **peer**：appear.

82 hard by：nearby.

86 Your grandfather：Henry's great-grandfather，Edward III. **an 't**：if it.

89 prave pattle：brave battle，指 Battle of Crécy，1346.

91—92 is remember'd of it：remembers it.

where leeks did grow, wearing leeks in their Monmouth caps; which, your majesty knows, to this hour is an honorable padge of the service; and I do pelieve your majesty takes no scorn to wear the leek upon Saint Tavy's day.

KING HENRY.

I wear it for a memorable honor;
For I am Welsh, you know, good countryman.

FLUELLEN.

All the water in Wye cannot wash your majesty's Welsh plood out of your pody, I can tell you that: Got pless it, and preserve it, as long as it pleases his grace, and his majesty too!

KING HENRY.

Thanks, good my countryman.

FLUELLEN.

By Cheshu, I am your majesty's countryman, I care not who know it; I will confess it to all the 'orld: I need not to be ashamed of your majesty, praised be Got, so long as your majesty is an honest man.

KING HENRY.

God keep me so! — Our heralds go with him:
Bring me just notice of the numbers dead
On both our parts. — Call yonder fellow hither.

[*Points to* WILLIAMS. *Exeunt* HERALDS *with* MONTJOY.]

DUKE OF EXETER.

Soldier, you must come to the king.

KING HENRY.

Soldier, why wear'st thou that glove in thy cap?

MICHAEL WILLIAMS.

An't please your majesty, 'tis the gage of one that I should fight withal, if he be alive.

KING HENRY.

93 leeks：the floral symbol of Wales. **Monmouth**：Henry V 的诞生地，曾被认为是威尔士的一部分，故 Henry V 有时自称是威尔士人。

95 padge：badge. **service**：military service. **pelieve**：believe.

96—97 Saint Tavy's day：March 1，Saint David's day，anniversary of the victory of the Welsh over the Saxons.

101 plood：blood. **pody**：body.

106—107 need not to be：needn't be.

108 honest：honorable.

109 him：Montjoy.

110 just notice：exact information.

114 gage：pledge.

An Englishman?

MICHAEL WILLIAMS.

An't please your majesty, a rascal that swagger'd with me last night; who, if alive, and ever dare to challenge this glove, I have sworn to take him a box o'th'ear: or if I can see my glove in his cap, which he swore, as he was a soldier, he would wear if alive, I will strike it out soundly.

KING HENRY.

What think you, Captain Fluellen? is it fit this soldier keep his oath?

FLUELLEN.

He is a craven and a villain else, an't please your majest, in my conscience.

KING HENRY.

It may be his enemy is a gentleman of great sort, quite from the answer of his degree.

FLUELLEN.

Though he be as goot a gentleman as the tevil is, as Lucifer and Belzebub himself, it is necessary, look your Grace, that he keep his vow and his oath: if he be perjured, see you now, his reputation is as arrant a villain and a Jack-sauce, as ever his plack shoe trod upon Got's ground and his earth, in my conscience, la.

KING HENRY.

Then keep thy vow, sirrah, when thou meet'st the fellow.

MICHAEL WILLIAMS.

So I will, my liege, as I live.

KING HENRY.

Who servest thou under?

MICHAEL WILLIAMS.

Under Captain Gower, my liege.

FLUELLEN.

Gower is a goot captain, and is goot knowledge and lit-

117 swagger'd with me: bandied words with me.

118 if alive: if he should still live.

119 take him a box o' th' ear: give him a box on the ear.

123 this soldier: the soldier who had William's other glove, in other words, King Henry V.

125 craven: coward. **else**: otherwise; if (he does) not (keep his oath).

126 conscience: conviction.

127 of great sort: of high rank.

128 quite from the answer of his degree: from=away from; answer=corresponding action; 意思是 debarred by the rules of the duel of responding only to a challenge from a person of his own rank.

129 as goot (good) a gentleman as the tevil (devil) is: a proverbial expression.

129—130 Lucifer:《圣经·旧约·以赛亚书》第 14 章 11 节,"明亮之星,据说是魔鬼撒旦(Satna)从天坠落之前的名字。"

130 Belzebub (Beelzebub):《圣经·新约·马太福音》第 12 章 24 节,鬼王别西卜。

132 perjured: forsworn. **arrant**: vile.

133 Jack-sauce: Saucy Jack; impudent fellow. ("Jack" is often used by Shakespeare as a term of contempt.)

134 la: an exclamation used to call attention to an emphatic statement.

139 is goot knowledge: has good knowledge.

eratured in the wars.

KING HENRY.

Call him hither to me, soldier.

MICHAEL WILLIAMS.

I will, my liege. [*Exit.*

KING HENRY.

Here, Fluellen; wear thou this favor for me, and stick it in thy cap: when Alençon and myself were down together, I pluckt this glove from his helm: if any man challenge this, he is a friend to Alençon , and an enemy to our person; if thou encounter any such, apprehend him, and thou dost me love.

FLUELLEN.

Your Grace does me as great honors as can be desired in the hearts of his subjects: I would fain see the man, that has but two legs, that shall find himself aggriefed at this glove; that is all; but I would fain see it once, an please Got of his grace that I might see.

KING HENRY.

Know'st thou Gower?

FLUELLEN.

He is my dear friend, an please you.

KING HENRY.

Pray thee, go seek him, and bring him to my tent.

FLUELLEN.

I will fetch him. [*Exit.*

KING HENRY.

My Lord of Warwick, and my brother Gloster,
Follow fluellen closely at the heels:
The glove which I have given him for a favor
May haply purchase him a box o'th'ear;
It is the soldier's; I, by bargain, should
Wear it myself. Follow, good cousin Warwick:
If that the soldier strike him, — as I judge

139—140 literatured：learned.

144 Alençon：John，the first Duke of Alençon，据传说他和 King Henry V 肉搏占上风，被 Henry 的侍从所杀。

144—145 down together：扭打在地。

150 fain：gladly；willingly.

151 aggriefed：aggrieved；afflicted.

152 at：on account of.

153 an please：if it pleases.

161 haply：perhaps. **purchase**：get；earn.

164 If that：If. **as**：sine.

By his blunt bearing, he will keep his word, —
Some sudden mischief may arise of it;
For I do know Fluellen valiant,
And, toucht with choler, hot as gunpowder,
And quickly will return an injury:
Follow, and see there be no harm between them. —
Go you with me, uncle of Exeter. [*Exeunt*.

SCENE VIII

Before KING HENRY'S *pavilion*.

Enter GOWER *and* WILLIAMS.

MICHAEL WILLIAMS.

I warrant it is to knight you, captain.

Enter FLUELLEN.

FLUELLEN.

Got's will and his pleasure, captain, I peseech you now, come apace to the king: there is more goot toward you peradventure than is in your knowledge to dream of.

MICHAEL WILLIAMS.

Sir, know you this glove?

FLUELLEN.

Know the glove! I know the glove is a glove.

MICHAEL WILLIAMS.

I know this; and thus I challenge it. [*Strikes him*.

FLUELLEN.

'Splood, an arrant traitor as any's in the universal'orld, or in France, or in England!

GOWER.

How now, sir! you villain!

MICHAEL WILLIAMS.

Do you think I'll be forsworn?

FLUELLEN.

166 of: from.

168 choler: 中世纪认为人有四种脾性(humors):phlegm, blood, choler 和 black bile, 带有 choler 者天性易怒。

169 will return: 省略主语 he.

IV. viii

1 knight (*v.*): 封为爵士或骑士。

2 peseech: beseech.

3 apace: quickly.

8 'Splood: God's blood (a mild oath).

11 be forsworn: break my oath.

Stand away, Captain Gower; I will give treason his payment into plows, I warrant you.

MICHAEL WILLIAMS.

I am no traitor.

FLUELLEN.

That's a lie in thy throat. — I charge you in his majesty's name, apprehend him: he's a friend of the Duke Alençon's.

Enter WARWICK *and* GLOSTER.

EARL OF WARWICK.

How now, how now! what's the matter?

FLUELLEN.

My Lord of Warwick, here is — praised be Got for it! — a most contagious treason come to light, look you, as you shall desire in a summer's day. — Here is his majesty.

Enter KING HENRY *and* EXETER.

KING HENRY.

How now! what's the matter?

FLUELLEN.

My liege, here is a villain and a traitor, that, look your Grace, has struck the glove which your majesty is take out of the helmet of Alençon.

MICHAEL WILLIAMS.

My liege, this was my glove; here is the fellow of it; and he that I gave it to in change promised to wear it in his cap: I promised to strike him, if he did: I met this man with my glove in his cap, and I have been as good as my word.

FLUELLEN.

Your majesty hear now, saving your majesty's manhood, what an arrant, rascally, beggarly, lousy knave it is: I hope your majesty is pear me testimony, and witness, and will avouchment, that this is the glove of Alençon,

13 into plows：in two blows.

15 lie in thy throat：说人撒谎是极大污辱，会引起决斗。

20 contagious：poisonous；noxious.

25 is take：has taken，他的英语不合语法。

27 fellow：the other one of the same pair.

28 in change：in exchange.

32—33 saving your majesty's manhood：an apology for being plain-spoken.

34 is pear：will bear.

35 avouchment：affirm.

that your majesty is give me, in your conscience, now.

KING HENRY.

Give me thy glove, soldier: look, here is the fellow of it.
'Twas I, indeed, thou promised'st to strike;
And thou hast given me most bitter terms.

FLUELLEN.

And please your majesty, let his neck answer for it, if there is any martial law in the 'orld.

KING HENRY.

How canst thou make me satisfaction?

MICHAEL WILLIAMS.

All offences, my liege, come from the heart: never came any from mine that might offend your majesty.

KING HENRY.

It was ourself thou didst abuse.

MICHAEL WILLIAMS.

Your majesty came not like yourself: you appear'd to me but as a common man; witness the night, your garments, your lowliness; and what your highness suffer'd under that shape, I beseech you take it for your own fault, and not mine: for had you been as I took you for, I made no offence; therefore, I beseech your highness, pardon me.

KING HENRY.

Here, uncle Exeter, fill this glove with crowns,
And give it to this fellow. — Keep it, fellow;
And wear it for an honor in thy cap
Till I do challenge it. — give him the crowns: —
And, captain, you must needs be friends with him.

FLUELLEN.

By this day and this light, the fellow has mettle enough in his pelly. — Hold, there is twelve pence for you; and I pray you to serve Got, and keep you out of prawls, and prabbles, and quarrels, and dissensions, and, I warrant

36 **is give**: has given.
39 **bitter terms**: bitter words; insults.
44 **any from mine**: anything from my heart.
47 **witness**: considering.
48 **lowliness**: humble bearing.
59 **pelly**: belly.
60 **prawls**: brawls.
61 **prabbles**: squabbles; quarrels.

you, it is the petter for you.

MICHAEL WILLIAMS.

I will none of your money.

FLUELLEN.

It is with a goot will; I can tell you, it will serve you to mend your shoes: come, wherefore should you be so pashful? Your shoes is not so goot: 'tis a goot silling, I warrant you, or I will change it.

Enter an English HERALD

KING HENRY.

Now, herald, — are the dead number'd?

HERALD.

Here is the number of the slaughter'd French.

[*Delivers a paper*.

KING HENRY.

What prisoners of good sort are taken, uncle?

DUKE OF EXETER.

Charles duke of Orleans, nephew to the king;
John duke of Bourbon, and Lord Bouciqualt;
Of other lords and barons, knights and squires,
Full fifteen hundred, besides common men.

KING HENRY.

This note doth tell me of ten thousand French
That in the field lie slain: of princes, in this number.
And nobles bearing banners, there lie dead
One hundred twenty-six: added to these,
Of knights, esquires, and gallant gentlemen,
Eight thousand and four hundred; of the which,
Five hundred were but yesterday dubb'd knights:
So that, in these ten thousand they have lost,
There are but sixteen hundred mercenaries;
The rest are princes, barons, lords, knights, squires,
And gentlemen of blood and quality.
The names of those their nobles that lie dead, —

66 **pashful**: bashful. **goot silling**: real shilling, no counterfeit.

70 **good sort**: high rank.

77 **banners**: standards on which their coats-of-arms were emblazoned.

81 **dubb'd**: to dub is (for the king) to make a person a knight by touching his shoulders with sword.

83 **mercenaries**: hired or paid soldiers.

Charles Delabreth, high-Constable of France;
Jaques of Chatillon, admiral of France;
The master of the cross-bows, Lord Rambures;
Great-master of France, the brave Sir Guiscard Dolphin;
John duke of Alençon; Antony duke of Brabant,
The brother to the Duke of Burgundy;
And Edward duke of Bar: of lusty earls,
Grandpré and Roussi, Fauconberg and Foix,
Beaumont and Marle, Vaudemont and Lestrale.
Here was a royal fellowship of death! —
Where is the number of our English dead? —

[HERALD *presents another paper*.]

Edward the duke of York, the Earl of Suffolk,
Sir Richard Ketly, Davy Gam, esquire;
None else of name; and of all other men
But five and twenty. — O God, Thy arm was here;
And not to us, but to Thy arm alone,
Ascribe we all! — When, without stratagem,
But in plain shock and even play of battle,
Was ever known so great and little loss
On one part and on th' other? — Take it, God,
For it is only Thine!

DUKE OF EXETER.

'Tis wonderful!

KING HENRY.

Come, go we in procession to the village:
And be it death proclaimed through our host
To boast of this, or take that praise from God
Which is His only.

FLUELLEN.

Is it not lawful, an please your majesty, to tell how many is kill'd?

KING HENRY.

Yes, captain; but with this acknowledgement,

93 lusty: vigorous.

100 of name: of distinguished reputation.

104 shock: combat. **even**: direct; straightforward.

109—110 be it death… to boast… or take: to boast or take (appropriate) … would mean death.

That God fought for us.

FLUELLEN.

Yes, my conscience, He did us great goot.

KING HENRY.

Do we all holy rites:
Let there be sung *Non nobis* and *Te Deum*.
The dead with charity enclosed in clay,
We'll then to Calais; and to England then;
Where ne'er from France arrived more happy men.

[*Exeunt*.

118 **Non nobis**："Not unto us",《圣经·旧约·诗篇》第 115 篇,意思是荣誉不归我们,而归上帝。 **Te Deum**：an old Christian hymn beginning with "Te Deum laudamus (we praise thee, O God)".

119 **enclosed in clay**：buried.

121 Never happier men would arrive in England from France.

ACT V PROLOGUE

Enter CHORUS.

CHORUS.

Vouchsafe to those that have not read the story,
That I may prompt them: and of such as have,
I humbly pray them to admit th'excuse
Of time, of numbers, and due course of things,
Which cannot in their huge and proper life
Be here presented. Now we bear the king
Towards Calais: grant him there; there seen,
Heave him away upon your winged thoughts
Athwart the sea. Behold, the English beach
Pales in the flood with men, with wives, and boys,
Whose shouts and claps out-voice the deep-mouth'd sea,
Which, like a mighty whiffler 'fore the king,
Seems to prepare his way: so let him land;
And solemnly see him set on to London.
So swift a pace hath thought, that even now
You may imagine him upon Blackheath;
Where that his lords desire him to have borne
His bruised helmet and his bended sword
Before him through the city: he forbids it,
Being free from vainness and self-glorious pride;
Giving full trophy, signal, and ostent,
Quite from himself to God. But now behold,
In the quick forge and working-house of thought,
How London doth pour out her citizens!
The mayor, and all his brethren, in best sort, —
Like to the senators of th' antique Rome,
With the plebeians swarming at their heels,—

V. Prologue 第五幕开场白。

Chorus：This chorus jumps from October 29，1415，when Henry was at Calais (line 6,7) to August 1，1417，the date of his 'back return again to France (lines 39—43)'，and does not say anything about his second campaign，which lasted about four years，and was brought to a close by the Anglo-French treaty of Troyes in 1420.

1 **Vouchsafe**：allow me.

2 **of such as have**：as for those who have (read the story).

9 **Athwart**：Across.

10 **Pales in**：Encircles；Fences in.

11 **claps**：clappings. **out-voice**：sound louder than. **deep-mouth'd**：loud and sonorous.

12 **whiffler**：official who walks first in royal procession to clear the way.

14 **solemnly**：ceremoniously.

16 **Blackheath**：伦敦东，泰晤士河南岸一高地，在今格林威治附近。

17 **Where that**：Where. **to have borne**：to have (his bruised helmet and his bent sword) borne.

21 **Giving**：Attributing. **signal**：sign of victory. **ostent**：external show.

23 **working-house**：workshop. **thought**：imagination.

25 **brethren**：colleagues. **in best sort**：in their best formalities.

26 **Like to**：like. **th' antique**：the ancient.

Go forth, and fetch their conquering Cæsar in:
As, by a lower but loving likelihood,
Were now the general of our gracious empress —
As in good time he may — from Ireland coming,
Bringing rebellion broached on his sword,
How many would the peaceful city quit,
To welcome him! much more, and much more cause,
Did they this Harry. Now in London place him; —
As yet the lamentation of the French
Invites the King of England's stay at home; —
The emperor's coming in behalf of France,
To order peace between them; — and omit
All the occurrences, whatever chanced,
Till Harry's back-return again to France:
There must we bring him; and myself have play'd
The interim, by remembering you 'tis past.
Then brook abridgement; and your eyes advance,
After your thoughts, straight back again to France.

[*Exit*.

SCENE I

France. The English camp.

Enter FLUELLEN *and* GOWER.

GOWER.

Nay, that's right; but why wear you your leek to-day? Saint Davy's day is past.

FLUELLEN.

There is occasions and causes why and wherefore in all things: I will tell you, asse my friend, Captain Gower: — the rascally, scald, peggarly, lousy, pragging knave, Pistol, — which you and yourself, and all the' orld, know to be no petter than a fellow, look you now, of no mer-

29 by a lower…likelihood：on the probable occasion of an event of inferior importance，but much cherished.

30 the general：the Earl of Essex. **our gracious empress**：Queen Elizabeth I. 1599 年 3 月底女王派宠臣埃塞克斯伯爵二世出征爱尔兰平叛。6 月底失败。9 月他擅自无功返回，还曾同叛军首领秘密接触，顿时失宠。1601 年谋叛被处死。因此这段台词创作时间可确定为 1599 年 4 月至 6 月之间。这是莎剧中最明显的提到时事的例子。

32 broached：spitted.

34—35 With much more cause they welcomed this Henry.

38 The emperor：the German emperor Sigismund，who was married to Henry's second cousin，came to London in May，1416，to mediate between Henry and the French king，Charles VI.

39 order：arrange.

41 back-return again：return.

43 remembering：reminding.

44 brook abridgement：tolerate this omission.

45 After：According to.

V. i

4 asse：as.

5 scald：scurvy；scabby. **peggarly**：beggarly. **pragging**：bragging.

6 which：whom.

7 petter：better.

its, — he is come to me, and prings me pread and salt yesterday, look you, and pid me eat my leek: it was in a place where I could not preed no contention with him; but I will be so pold as to wear it in my cap till I see him once again, and then I will tell him a little piece of my desires.

GOWER.

Why, here he comes, swelling like a turkeycock.

FLUELLEN.

'Tis no matter for his swellings nor his turkeycocks.

Enter PISTOL.

Got pless you, Auncient Pistol! you scurvy, lousy knave, Got pless you!

PISTOL.

Ha! art thou bedlam? dost thou thirst, base Trojan,
To have me fold up Parca's fatal web?
Hence! I am qualmish at the smell of leek.

FLUELLEN.

I peseech you heartily, scurvy, lousy knave, at my desires, and my requests, and my petitions, to eat, look you, this leek: because, look you, you do not love it, nor your affections, and your appetites, and your degestions, does not agree with it, I would desire you to eat it.

PISTOL.

Not for Cadwallader and all his goats.

FLUELLEN.

There is one goat for you. [*Strikes him*.] Will you be so goot, scald knave, as eat it?

PISTOL.

Base Trojan, thou shalt die.

FLUELLEN.

You say very true, scald knave, — when Got's will is: I will desire you to live in the mean time, and eat your victuals: come, there is sauce for it. [*Strikes him again*.

7—8 fellow…of no merits: worthless fellow.

8 is come: come. **prings**: brought. **pread**: bread.

9 pid: bade.

10 preed (breed) **contention**: have it out.

11 pold: bold.

12—13 tell him a little piece of my desires: give him a little piece of my mind.

14 swelling: inflated with pride.

15 'Tis no matter for: Never mind.

18 bedlam: mad, a corruption of "Bethlehem", a London hospital for the insane. **thirst**: desire. **Trojan**: dissolute fellow, a common term of opprobrium.

19 fold up Parca's fatal web: the Parcae (the fates) 命运女神，纺的线代表人的生命; therefore, to fold up their web is to cut the thread of life.

20 qualmish: squeamish.

26 Cadwallader: last of the Celtic kings, 6th century.

28 eat: 前省略 to.

You call'd me yesterday mountain-squire; but I will make you to-day a squire of low degree. I pray you, fall to: if you can mock a leek, you can eat a leek.

GOWER.

Enough, captain: you have astonisht him.

FLUELLEN.

I say, I will make him eat some part of my leek, or I will peat his pate four days. — Pite, I pray you; it is goot for your green wound and your ploody coxcomb.

PISTOL.

Must I bite?

FLUELLEN.

Yes, certainly, and out of doubt, and out of question too. and ambiguities.

PISTOL.

By this leek, I will most horrible revenge:
I eat and eat, I swear —

FLUELLEN.

Eat, I pray you: will you have some more sauce to your leek? there is not enough leek to swear by.

PISTOL.

Quiet thy cudgel; thou dost see I eat.

FLUELLEN.

Much goot do you, scald knave, heartily. Nay, pray you, throw none away; the skin is goot for your proken coxcomb. When you take occasions to see leeks hereafter, I pray you, mock at' em; that is all.

PISTOL.

Good.

FLUELLEN.

Ay, leeks is goot: — hold you, there is a groat to heal your pate.

PISTOL.

Me a groat!

33 **mountain-squire**：a man with worthless land；hence，a poor man.

34 **low**：① mean；base；② down from the mountain.

34—35 **fall to**：begin eating（leek）.

36 **astonisht**（astonished）：stunned.

38 **peat**：beat. **Pite**：Bite.

39 **green**：fresh；raw. **coxcomb**：head.

41 **out of doubt**：without doubt.

42 **ambiguities**：out of（without）ambiguities.

47 **Quiet**：Quit；Lay down.

49 **proken**：broken.

50 **take occasions**：have opportunity.

53 **groat**：值四便士的小银币。

FLUELLEN.

Yes, verily and in truth, you shall take it; or I have another leek in my pocket, which you shall eat.

PISTOL.

I take thy groat in earnest of revenge.

FLUELLEN.

If I owe you any thing, I will pay you in cudgels; you shall be a woodmonger, and buy nothing of me but cugels. Got b'wi'you, and keep you, and heal your pate. [*Exit*.

PISTOL.

All hell shall stir for this.

GOWER.

Go, go; you are a counterfeit cowardly knave. Will you mock at an ancient tradition, — begun upon an honorable respect, and worn as a memorable trophy of predeceased valor, — and dare not avouch in your deeds any of your words? I have seen you gleeking and galling at this gentleman twice or thrice. You thought, because he could not speak English in the native garb, he could not therefore handle an English cudgel: you find it otherwise; and henceforth let a Welsh correction teach you a good English condition. Fare ye well. [*Exit*.

PISTOL.

Doth Fortune play the huswife with me now?
News have I, that my Nell is dead i'th' spital
Of malady of France;
And there my rendezvous is quite cut off.
Old I do wax; and from my weary limbs
Honor is cudgell'd. Well, bawd will I turn,
And something lean to cutpurse of quick hand.
To England will I steal, and there I' ll steal:
And patches will I get unto these scars,

58 **earnest**：定钱。作为报复的定钱。

60 **woodmonger**：seller of wood.

62 Pistol's threat of taking revenge.

64—65 **upon an honorable respect**：for an honorable reason.

65—66 **predeceased**：previously extinct.

66 **avouch**：back up；live up to.

67 **gleeking and galling**：gibing and scoffing.

69 **garb**：fashion.

71 **correction**：punishment；chastisement.

72 **condition**：disposition.

73 **huswife**：hussy；light woman.

74 **Nell**：应作 Doll，即 Mistress Quickly，Pistol 的妻子，见第 2 幕 1 场。 **I' th' spital**：in the hospital.

75 **malady of France**：venereal disease.

76 **rendezvous**：retreat；refuge.

77 **wax**：grow.

78 **cudgell'd**：produced by a cudgel. **bawd**：procurer；keeper of a brothel.

79 **something lean to**：something like.

80 **steal**：a play of words：the first 'steal' means to go in a stealthy manner，the second 'pilfer'.

81 **patches**：膏药。

And swear I got them in the Gallia wars. [*Exit*.

SCENE II

France. The French KING'S *palace.*

Enter, at one door, KING HENRY, BEDFORD, GLOSTER, EXETER, WARWICK, WESTMORELAND, *and other* LORDS; *at another*, *the French* KING, QUEEN ISABEL, *the* PRINCESS KATHARINE, ALICE, *other* LADIES, *and* LORDS; *the* DUKE OF BURGUNDY, *and his* TRAIN.

KING HENRY.

Peace to this meeting, wherefore we are met!
Unto our brother France, and to our sister,
Health and fair time of day; — joy and good wishes
To our most fair and princely cousin Katharine; —
And as a branch and member of this royalty,
By whom this great assembly is contrived,
We do salute you, Duke of Burgundy;—
And, princes French, and peers, health to you all!

FRENCH KING.

Right joyous are we to behold your face,
Most worthy brother England; fairly met: —
So are you, princes English, every one.

QUEEN ISABEL.

So happy be the issue, brother England,
Of this good day and of this gracious meeting,
As we are now glad to behold your eyes;
Yours eyes, which hitherto have borne in them
Against the French, that met them in their bent,
The fatal balls of murdering basilisks:
The venom of such looks, we fairly hope,
Have lost their quality; and that this day
Shall change all griefs and quarrels into love.

82 Gallia：French.

V. ii

1 meeting：in Troyes，France，on May 21，1420. **wherefore**：for which (peace).

2 France：the French king，Charles VI. **our sister**：the French queen，Isabella of Bavaria，时年 50 岁。

4 princely：royal；regal. **Katharine**：时年近 20 岁。

6 contrived：arranged.

12 issue：outcome.

15—17 此句核心为 Your eyes have borne in them the balls of…

16 that：who. **them**：your eyes. **bent**：① inclination of eyes；② inclination of a cannon.

17 basilisks：① 目光能杀人的非洲沙漠蛇怪；② 一种火炮。**balls**：① eyes；② cannon-balls.

18 fairly：respectfully.

18—19 核心部分为 we hope that the venom has… and that this day… has 由于接近 looks 而变成 have.

KING HENRY.

To cry amen to that, thus we appear.

QUEEN ISABEL.

You English princes all, I do salute you.

DUKE OF BURGUNDY.

My duty to you both, on equal love,
Great Kings of France and England! That I have labor'd,
With all my wits, my pains, and strong endeavors,
To bring your most imperial majesties
Unto this bar and royal interview,
Your mightiness on both parts best can witness.
since, then, my office hath so far prevail'd
That, face to face and royal eye to eye,
You have congreeted, let it not disgrace me,
If I demand, before this royal view,
What rub or what impediment there is,
Why that the naked, poor, and mangled Peace,
Dear nurse of arts, plenties, and joyful births,
Should not, in this best garden of the world,
Our fertile France, put up her lovely visage?
Alas, she hath from France too long been chased!
And all her husbandry doth lie on heaps,
Corrupting in its own fertility.
Her vine, the merry cheerer of the heart,
Unpruned dies; her hedges even-pleacht,
Like prisoners wildly overgrown with hair,
Put forth disorder'd twigs; her fallow leas
The darnel, hemlock, and rank fumitory,
Do root upon, while that the coulter rusts,
That should deracinate such savagery;
The even mead, that erst brought sweetly forth
The freckled cowslip, burnet, and green clover,
Wanting the scythe, all uncorrected, rank,

21 amen：so be it，基督教祈祷中的赞同词，阿门。

23 on equal love：proceeding from equal love for both of you.

25 pains：troubles；efforts.

27 bar：tribunal.

28 mightiness：mightinesses，s 音之后的复数 es 常略去。

31 congreeted：greeted each other. 莎士比亚临时创造的词之一。**disgrace me**：put me out of favor.

32 demand：ask. **view**：presence.

33 rub：滚球戏中地面不平之处；hindrance.

34 Why that：Why. **mangled**：伤残的。 **Peace**：这里把"和平"喻为女神。

34—37 句的核心为 Why should Peace not put up her visage?

37 put up：show；display.

38 she：Peace.

39 her：从语法上讲是 of Peace，实际上是 of France. **husbandry**：crops. **on heaps**：in a fallen or prostrate mass；in ruins.

41 vine：grapevines.

42 even-pleacht：evenly interwoven.

44 fallow leas：meadows lying fallow（untilled）.

45 darnel：毒麦。 **hemlock**：毒芹。 **rank fumitory**：可烧烟熏虫的蓝堇。

46 root upon：take root in. **while that**：while. **coulter**：plow blade，犁铧。

47 deracinate：uproot. **savagery**：wild vegetation.

48 even：flat. **mead**：meadow. **erst**：erstwhile；formerly.

49 burnet：开棕色花的地榆。

50 Wanting：lacking.

Conceives by idleness, and nothing teems
But hateful docks, rough thistles, kecksies, burs,
Losing both beauty and utility.
And as our vineyards, fallows, meads, and hedges,
Defective in their natures, grow to wildness,
Even so our houses, and ourselves and children,
Have lost, or do not learn for want of time,
The sciences that should become our country;
But grow, like savages, — as soldiers will,
That nothing do but meditate on blood, —
To swearing, and stern looks, diffused attire,
And every thing that seems unnatural.
Which to reduce into our former favor,
You are assembled: and my speech entreats
That I may know the let, why gentle Peace
Should not expel these inconveniences,
And bless us with her former qualities.

KING HENRY.

If, Duke of Burgundy, you would the peace,
Whose want gives growth to th' imperfections
Which you have cited, you must buy that peace
With full accord to all our just demands;
Whose tenors and particular effects
You have, enscheduled briefly, in your hands.

DUKE OF BURGUNDY.

The king hath heard them; to the which as yet
There is no answer made.

KING HENRY.

Well, then, the peace,
Which you before so urged, lies in his answer.

FRENCH KING.

I have but with a cursorary eye
O'erglanced the articles: pleaseth your Grace
To appoint some of your council presently

51 **Conceives by idleness**: Breeds through idleness. **teems**: brings forth.

52 **docks**: 酸模属草。 **kecksies**: 长伞形花的野草。

55 **Defective in their natures**: defective because they are not cultivated and left in their natural state.

58 **sciences**: branches of knowledge.

61 **diffused**: disordered.

63 **reduce into**: restore to. **favor**: charming appearance.

65 **let**: hindrance.

68 **would**: desire.

72 **tenors**: substance. **effects**: stipulations.

73 **enscheduled**: listed.

77 **cursorary**: cursory; hasty.

78 **O'erglanced**: glanced over. **pleaseth**: if it pleases.

79 **council**: 国王的御前参议;枢密院。 **presently**: immediately.

To sit with us once more, with better heed
To re-survey them, we will suddenly
Pass our accept and peremptory answer.

KING HENRY.

Brother, we shall. — Go, uncle Exeter, —
And brother Clarence, — and you, brother Gloster,—
Warwick, — and Huntingdon, —go with the king;
And take with you free power to ratify,
Augment, or alter, as your wisdoms best
Shall see advantageable for our dignity,
Any thing in or out of our demands;
And we'll consign thereto. — Will you, fair sister,
Go with the princes, or stay here with us?

QUEEN ISABEL.

Our gracious brother, I will go with them:
Haply a woman's voice may do some good,
When articles too nicely urged be stood on.

KING HENRY.

Yet leave our cousin Katharine here with us:
She is our capital demand, comprised
Within the fore-rank of our articles.

QUEEN ISABEL.

She hath good leave.

[*Exeunt all except* KING HENRY, KATHARINE, *and* ALICE.

KING HENRY.

Fair Katharine, and most fair!
Will you vouchsafe to teach a soldier terms
Such as will enter at a lady's ear,
And plead his love-suit to her gentle heart?

KATHARINE.

Your majesty shall mock at me; I cannot speak your England.

KING HENRY.

81 **suddenly**：in no time；immediately.

82 **Pass…answer**：pronounce our accepted（i.e. adopted）and decisive answer.像 accept 这样以 t 音结尾的动词，过去分词词尾-ed 常略去。

87 **wisdoms**：当时抽象名词可有复数。

88 **advantageable**：advantageous.

90 **consign**：set one's seal，（hence）agree.

93 **Haply**：perhaps.

94 **nicely**：minutely. **stood on**：insisted upon.

96 **capital**：chief；principal.

99 **terms**：manner of speaking.

102 **shall**：would.

103 **England**：English. 她的英语中有很多错误，以后不一一指出。

O fair Katharine, if you will love me soundly with your French heart, I will be glad to hear you confess it brokenly with your English tongue. Do you like me, Kate?

KATHARINE.

Pardonnez-moi, I cannot tell vat is 'like me'.

KING HENRY.

An angel is like you, Kate, and you are like an angel.

KATHARINE.

Que dit-il? que je suis semblable à les anges?

ALICE.

Oui, vraiment, sauf votre grace, ainsi dit-il.

KING HENRY.

I said so, dear Katharine; and I must not blush to affirm it.

KATHARINE.

O bon Dieu! les langues des hommes sont pleines de tromperies.

KING HENRY.

What says she, fair one? that the tongues of men are full of deceits?

ALICE.

Oui, dat de tongues of de mans is be full of deceits — dat is de princess.

KING HENRY.

The princess is the better Englishwoman. I'faith, Kate, my wooing is fit for thy understanding: I am glad thou canst speak no better English; for, if thou couldst, thou wouldst find me such a plain king that thou wouldst think I had sold my farm to buy my crown. I know no ways to mince it in love, but directly to say, 'I love you:' then, if you urge me further than to say, 'Do you in faith?' I wear out my suit. Give me your answer; i'faith, do; and so clap hands and a bargain: how say you, lady?

104 soundly: perfectly (in antithesis with 'brokenly' which appears in the next line).

107 Pardonnez-moi: pardon me. **vat**: what.

109 What did he say? That I am like the angels?

110 Yes, truly, save your grace, so did he.

113—114 O good God, the tongues of men are full of deceits.

115 fair one: 对 Alice.

118 dat is de princess: that is what the princess says.

119 The princess…Englishwoman: Unlike the French who are prone to make and like compliments, Katharine is more of an English woman for saying so (recognizing his flattery for what it is).

124 mince it: speak with affected delicacy.

126 wear out my suit: have nothing further to say. "suit" is ①petition; courting; ② dress.

127 clap: strike (hands) reciprocally in token of a bargain.

KATHARINE.

Sauf votre honneur, me understand vell.

KING HENRY.

Marry, if you would put me to verses or to dance for your sake, Kate, why, you undid me: for the one, I have neither words nor measure; and for the other, I have no strength in measure, yet a reasonable measure in strength. If I could win a lady at leap-frog, or by vaulting into my saddle with my armor on my back, under the correction of bragging be it spoken, I should quickly leap into a wife. Or if I might buffet for my love, or bound my horse for her favors, I could lay on like a butcher, and sit like a jack-an-apes, never off. But, before God, Kate, I cannot look greenly, nor gasp out my eloquence, nor I have no cunning in protestation; only downright oaths, which I never use till urged, nor never break for urging. If thou canst love a fellow of this temper, Kate, whose face is not worth sun-burning, that never looks in his glass for love of any thing he sees there, — let thine eye be thy cook. I speak to thee plain soldier: if thou canst love me for this, take me; if not, to say to thee that I shall die, is true, — but for thy love, by the Lord, no; yet I love thee too. And while thou livest, dear Kate, take a fellow of plain and uncoin'd constancy; for he perforce must do thee right, because he hath not the gift to woo in other places: for these fellows of infinite tongue, that can rime themselves into ladies' favors, they do always reason themselves out again. What! a speaker is but a prater; a rime is but a ballad. A good leg will fall; a straight back will stoop; a black beard will turn white; a curl'd pate will grow bald; a fair face will wither; a full eye will wax hollow: but a good heart, Kate, is the sun and the moon; or, rather, the sun, and not the moon, —

129 **Sauf votre honneur**: save your honor.

131 **you undid me**: you would put me to shame.

132 **measure**: meter; 诗律。

132—133 **have no strength in**: be not good at.

133 **measure**: dance, especially grave or stately dance.

133—134 **measure in strength**: amount of strength.

135—136 **under the correction of**: with apologies for.

137 **buffet**: box; 拳击。

138 **bound**: cause to leap (or romp). **lay on**: punch.

139 **jack-an-apes**: pet monkey.

140 **greenly**: lovesick.

141 **cunning**: skill. **protestation**: solemn declaration.

142 **urged**: hard pressed (by circumstances).

143 **for urging**: in any contingency.

144 **is not worth sun-burning**: cannot be bettered or worsened by sunning.

146 **be thy cook**: dress your dish (i.e. me) to suit yourself.

146—147 **I speak to thee plain soldier**: I speak to you as a plain soldier.

148—149 **but for thy love**: but to die for your love.

150—151 **uncoin'd constancy**: genuine faithfulness. 'uncoined' = a piece of unstamped metal which cannot circulate in other places.

153 **infinite**: glib.

156 **fall**: fall away; shrink.

for it shines bright, and never changes, but keeps his course truly. If thou would have such a one, take me: and take me, take a soldier; take a soldier, take a king: and what say'st thou, then, to my love? speak, my fair, and fairly, I pray thee.

KATHARINE.

Is it possible dat I sould love de enemy of France?

KING HENRY.

No; it is not possible you should love the enemy of France, Kate: but, in loving me, you should love the friend of France; for I love France so well, that I will not part with a village of it; I will have it all mine: and, Kate, when France is mine and I am yours, then yours is France and you are mine.

KATHARINE.

I cannot tell vat is dat.

KING HENRY.

No, Kate? I will tell thee in French; which I an sure will hang upon my tongue like a new-married wife about her husband's neck, hardly to be shook off. *Je quand sur le possession de France, et quand vous avez le possession de moi*, — let me see, what then? Saint Denis be my speed! — *donc votre est France et vous êtes mienne*. It is as easy for me, Kate, to conquer the kingdom, as to speak so much more French: I shall never move thee in French, unless it be to laugh at me.

KATHARINE.

Sauf votre honneur, le Français que vous parlez, il est meilleur que l'Anglais lequel je parle.

KING HENRY.

No, faith, is't not, Kate: but thy speaking of my tongue, and I thine, most truly-falsely, must needs be granted to be much at one. But, Kate, dost thou understand thus much English, — Canst thou love me?

165 **fairly**：favorably.

176 **shook**：shaken.

176—178 法语，when I am in possession of France and you in possession of me… then yours is France and you are mine.

178—179 **Saint Denis be my speed**：Saint Denis（the patron saint of France）help me. speed=fortune.

183—184 Save your honor，the French you speak is better than the English I speak.

186 **truly-falsely**：in true intention but faulty language.

187 **at one**：alike.

KATHARINE.

I cannot tell.

KING HENRY.

Can any of your neighbors tell, Kate? I'll ask them. Come, I know thou lovest me: and at night, when you come into your closet, you'll question this gentlewoman about me; and I know, Kate, you will to her dispraise those parts in me that you love with your heart: but, good Kate, mock me mercifully; the rather, gentle princess, because I love thee cruelly. If ever thou beest mine, Kate, — as I have a saving faith within me tells me thou shalt, — I get thee with scambling, and thou must therefore needs prove a good soldier-breeder: shall not thou and I, between Saint Denis and Saint George, compound a boy, half French, half English, that shll go to Constantinople and take the Turk by the beard? shall we not? what say'st thou, my fair flower-de-luce?

KATHARINE.

I do not know dat.

KING HENRY.

No; 'tis hereafter to know, but now to promise: do but now promise, Kate, you will endeavor for your French part of such a boy; and for my English moiety take the word of a king and a bachelor. How answer you, *la plus belle Katharine du monde, mon très-chère et devin déesse*?

KATHARINE.

Your majestee ave *fausse* French enough to deceive de most *sage demoiselle* dat is *en France*.

KING HENRY.

Now, fie upon my false French! By mine honor, in true English, I love thee, Kate: by which honor I dare not swear thou lovest me; yet my blood begins to flatter me that thou dost, notwithstanding the poor and untemper-

192 closet: bedchamber.

193 dispraise: disparage; censure.

196 cruelly: excessively. **beest**: be.

197 saving: comforting.

198 scambling: scrambling; struggling (in the war).

200 Saint Denis and Saint George: the patron saint of France and that of England. **compound**: form; make up.

201—202 go to Constantinople and take the Turk by the beard: 即在十字军东征中获胜,从土耳其国王手下解放耶路撒冷。奥斯曼帝国以君士坦丁堡为都。

203 flower-de-luce: fleur-de-lis, or iris(鸢尾花), the royal emblem of France.

207 moiety: half; share.

209—210 法语, the most beautiful Katharine of the world, my very dear and divine goddess.

211—212 Your majesty have false French enough to deceive the most clever girl that is in France.

ing effect of my visage. Now, beshrew my father's ambition! he was thinking of civil wars when he got me: therefore was I created with a stubborn outside, with an aspect of iron, that, when I come to woo ladies, I fright them. But, in faith, Kate, the elder I wax, the better I shall appear: my comfort is, that old age, that ill layer-up of beauty, can do no more spoil upon my face: thou hast me, if thou hast me, at the worst; and thou shalt wear me, if thou wear me, better and better: — and therefore tell me, most fair Katharine, will you have me? Put off your maiden blushes; avouch the thoughts of your heart with the looks of an empress; take me by the hand, and say, 'Harry of England, I am thine:' which word thou shalt no sooner bless mine ear withal, but I will tell thee aloud, 'England is thine, Ireland is thine, France is thine, and Henry Plantagenet is thine;' who, though I speak it before his face, if he be not fellow with the best king, thou shalt find the best king of good fellows. Come, your answer in broken music, — for thy voice is music, and thy English broken; therefore, queen of all, Katharine, break thy mind to me in broken English, — wilt thou have me?

KATHARINE.

Dat is as it sall please de *roi mon père*.

KING HENRY.

Nay, it will please him well, Kate, — it shall please him, Kate.

KATHARINE.

Den it sall also content me.

KING HENRY.

Upon that I kiss your hand, and I call you my queen.

KATHARINE.

Laissez, mon seigneur, laissez, laissez: ma foi, je ne veux point que vous abaissiez votre grandeur en baisant la

216—217 **untempering**：incapable of tempering or softening you.

217 **visage**：face. **beshrew**：curse.

218 **got**：begot.

219 **stubborn**：rough.

220 **that**：so that.

222 **layer-up**：preserver.

224 **wear**：bear or bear with.

230 **withal**：with. **but**：than.

232 **Plantagenet**：扫帚草王朝（旧译金雀花王朝）。 **who**：Henry V.

233 **fellow**：associate；equal.

234 **fellows**：people.

235 **broken music**：① halting，musical English；② music arranged in parts.

236—237 另一本作 queen of all Katharine.

237 **break**：reveal.

239 **sall**：shall. **de roi mon père**：the king，my father.

240 **shall**：is sure to.

main d'une votre indigne serviteur; excusez-moi, je vous supplie, mon très-puissant seigneur.

KING HNERY.

Then I will kiss your lips, Kate.

KATHARINE.

Les dames et demoiselles pour être baisées devant leur noces, il n'est pas la coutume de France.

KING HENRY.

Madam my interpreter, what says she?

ALICE.

Dat it is not de fashion *pour les* ladies of France, — I cannot tell vat is *baiser en Anglish.*

KING HENRY.

To kiss.

ALICE.

Your majestee *entendre* bettre *que moi.*

KING HENRY.

It is not a fashion for the maids in France to kiss before they are married, would she say?

ALICE.

Oui, vraiment.

KING HENRY.

O Kate, nice customs court'sy to great kings. Dear Kate, you and I cannot be confined within the weak list of a country's fashion: we are the makers of manners, Kate; and the liberty that follows our places stops the mouth of all find-faults, — as I will do yours for upholding the nice fashion of your country in denying me a kiss: therefore, patiently and yielding. [*Kissing her.*] You have witchcraft in your lips, Kate: there is more eloquence in a sugar touch of them than in the tongues of the French council; and they should sooner persuade Harry of England than a general petition of monarchs. — Here comes your father.

244—247 Laissez…seigneur: Let go, my lord, let go. let go. My faith, I do not wish that you should abuse your greatness in kissing the hand of one — your unworthy servant. Excuse me, I beg of you, my very powerful lord.

249—250 It is not the French custom for ladies and maids to be kissed before their marriages.

252 **pour**: for.

253 **baiser en Anglish**: kissing in English.

255 **entendre**: understand. **que moi**: than me.

258 Yes, truly.

259 **nice**: fastidious. **court'sy to**: bow to; submit to.

260 **weak list**: easily broken boundary.

262 **follows our places**: go along with our rank.

263 **find-faults**: faultfinders. **do yours**: stop your mouth.

264 **nice fashion**: fastidious custom.

265 **patiently and yielding**: be patient and yield.

Enter the French KING *and* QUEEN, BURGUNDY, BEDFORD, GLOSTER, EXETER, WESTMORELAND, WARWICK, *&c.*

DUKE OF BURGUNDY.

God save your majesty! my royal cousin, teach you our princess English?

KING HENRY.

I would have her learn, my fair cousin, how perfectly I love her; and that is good English.

DUKE OF BURGUNDY.

Is she not apt?

KING HENRY.

Our tongue is rough, coz, and my condition is not smooth; so that, having neither the voice nor the heart of flattery about me, I cannot so conjure up the spirit of love in her, that he will appear in his true likeness.

DUKE OF BURGUNDY.

Pardon the frankness of my mirth, if I answer you for that. If you would conjure in her. you must make a circle; if conjure up love in her in his true likeness, he must appear naked and blind. Can you blame her, then, being a maid yet rosed-over with the virgin crimson of modesty, if she deny the appearance of a naked blind boy in her naked seeing self? It were, my lord, a hard condition for a maid to consign to.

KING HENRY.

Yet they do wink and yield, — as love is blind and enforces.

DUKE OF BURGUNDY.

They are then excused, my lord, when they see not what they do.

KING HENRY.

Then, good my lord, teach your cousin to consent winking.

DUKE OF BURGUNDY.

271—272 teach you: Have you been teaching.

275 apt: quick to learn.

276 condition: disposition; character.

277 smooth: gentle.

278 conjure up: bring into existence as by magic.

279 he: love.

281—282 make a circle: ①施魔法时要在对象周围画一个圈；②送她戒指。

283 naked and blind: Cupid, the god of Love, is always pictured as a naked and blind boy.

284 rosed-over: colored rosy.

286 naked seeing self: open eye.

287 consign: agree.

288 they: maids. **wink**: shut their eyes.

288—289 enforces: compels.

I will wink on her to consent, my lord, if you will teach her to know my meaning: for maids, well summer'd and warm kept, are like flies at Bartholomew-tide, blind, though they have their eyes; and then they will endure handling, which before would not abide looking on.

KING HENRY.

This moral ties me over to time and a hot summer; and so I shall catch the fly, your cousin, in the latter end, and she must be blind too.

DUKE OF BURGUNDY.

As love is, my lord, before it loves.

KING HENRY.

It is so: and you may, some of you, thank love for my blindness, who cannot see many a fair French city for one fair French maid that stands in my way.

FRENCH KING.

Yes, my lord, you see them perspectively, the cities turn'd into a maid; for they are all girdled with maiden walls that war hath never enter'd.

KING HENRY.

Shall Kate be my wife?

FRENCH KING.

So please you.

KING HENRY.

I am content; so the maiden cities you talk of may wait on her: so the maid that stood in the way for my wish shall show me the way to my will.

FRENCH KING.

We have consented to all terms of reason.

KING HENRY.

Is 't so, my lords of England?

EARL OF WESTMORELAND.

The king hath granted every article:—
His daughter first; and then, in sequel, all,

295 summer'd: kept during the summer.

296 Bartholomew-tide: August 24, St. Bartholomew's Day, when the evenings begin to grow chilly and flies sluggish.

299 ties me over to time and a hot summer: obliges me to wait for some time and until a hot summer has passed.

300 in the latter end: in the end.

306 perspectively: in an optical delusion.

311—312 So the maiden cities… her: provided that she bring the cities with her (as a dowry, or, as her waiting maids).

312 for: of.

314 terms of reason: reasonable terms.

317 in sequel: in due succession.

According to their firm proposed natures.

DUKE OF EXETER.

Only, he hath not yet subscribed this:
Where your majesty demands, that the King of France, having any occasion to write for matter of grant, shall name your highness in this form and with this addition, in French, *Notre très-cher fils Henri, roi d'Angleterre, héritier de France*; and thus in Latin, *Præclarissimus filius noster Henricus, rex Angliæ, et hæres Franciæ*

FRENCH KING.

Nor this I have not, brother, so denied,
But your request shall make me let it pass.

KING HENRY.

I pray you, then, in love and dear alliance,
Let that one article rank with the rest;
And thereupon give me your daughter.

FRENCH KING.

Take her, fair son; and from her blood raise up
Issue to me; that the contending kingdoms
Of France and England, whose very shores look pale
With envy of each other's happiness,
May cease their hatred; and this dear conjunction
Plant neighborhood and christian-like accord
In their sweet bosoms, that never war advance
His bleeding sword 'twixt England and fair France.

ALL.

Amen!

KING HENRY.

Now, welcome, Kate; — and bear me witness all,
That here I kiss her as my sovereign queen. [*Flourish*.

QUEEN ISABEL.

God, the best maker of all marriages,
Combine your hearts in one, your realms in one!
As man and wife, being two, are one in love,

318 their firm proposed natures：in the exact form in which they were proposed.

319 subscribed：agreed to.

321 matter of grant：转让文书。

323—325 法文和拉丁文均为 our very dear son Henry，King of England and heir of France. 但拉丁文第一字 Præclarissimus（proclaim you）在有些版本里错成 Præcharissimus.

332 Issue：offspring.

335 dear conjunction：important union.

So be there 'twixt your kingdoms such a spousal,
That never may ill office, or fell jealousy,
Which troubles oft the bed of blessed marriage,
Thrust in between the paction of these kingdoms,
To make divorce of their incorporate league;
That English may as French, French Englishmen,
Receive each other! — God speak this Amen!

ALL.

Amen!

KING HENRY.

Prepare we for our marriage: — on which day,
My lord of Burgundy, we'll take your oath,
And all the peers', for surety of our leagues.
Then shall I swear to Kate, and you to me;
And may our oaths well kept and prosperous be!

[Sennet. *Exeunt*.]

345 **spousal**: marriage.

346 **ill office**: disservice. **fell**: cruel.

348 **paction**: compact; alliance.

349 **make divorce of**: separate. **incorporate** (*p.p.*): closely united.

350 **as**: acting in the spirit of.

353 **on which day**: on that day.

355 **for surety**: for guarantee.

357 **Sennet**: set of notes played on the trumpet or cornet as a signal for the approach or departure of a company or procession.

EPILOGUE

Enter CHORUS

CHORUS.

Thus far, with rough and all unable pen.
Our bending author hath pursued the story;
In little room confining mighty men,
Mangling by starts the full course of their glory.
Small time, but in that small, most greatly liv'd
This star of England: fortune made his sword;
By which the world's best garden he achieved,
And of it left his son imperial lord.
Henry the Sixth, in infant bands crown'd King
Of France and England, did this king succeed;
Whose state so many had the managing,
That they lost France, and made his England bleed:
Which oft our stage hath shown; and, for their sake,
In your fair minds let this acceptance take. [*Exit*.]

EPILOGUE 收场白，是一首十四行诗。

1 all unable：inept；impotent.

2 bending：① stooping to the audience's clemency；or ②bending under the weight of the subject.

4 by starts：by fits and starts；by a piecemeal presentation.

5 Small time：① the little time, about two hours, that was allotted to the performance of a play；or ②the short life-span of Henry V (1387—1422), who died at the age of 35.

7 the world's best garden：France (Burgundy's phrase at V. ii 36).

9 infant bands：swaddling clothes，他不到一岁时接位。

11 many had the managing：多人摄政。 **the managing**：the management of.

13 Which oft our stage hath shown：the three parts of Henry VI had already been very popular on the stage.

14 let this acceptance take：accept this play, too.

图书在版编目(CIP)数据

亨利五世 / (英)莎士比亚(Shakespeare, W.)著; 支荩忠注释.—北京:商务印书馆,2014(2016.3 重印)
(莎翁戏剧经典)
ISBN 978-7-100-09956-1

Ⅰ. ①亨… Ⅱ. ①莎… ②支… Ⅲ. ①英语—语言读物 ②剧本—英国—中世纪 Ⅳ. ①H319.4:I

中国版本图书馆 CIP 数据核字(2013)第 095850 号

莎翁戏剧经典

HĒNGLÌ WǓ SHÌ

亨 利 五 世

〔英〕威廉·莎士比亚 著

支荩忠 注释

商 务 印 书 馆 出 版

(北京王府井大街36号 邮政编码 100710)

商 务 印 书 馆 发 行

北 京 冠 中 印 刷 厂 印 刷

ISBN 978-7-100-09956-1

2014 年 8 月第 1 版　　开本 787×1092 1/32

2016 年 3 月北京第 2 次印刷　　印张 9½ 插页 1

定价: 29.00 元

(your bed Right next to your face Begin to make contact Closer closer closer to y

I had my wishes If I had my way I'd be all the time with you Each and everyday

b I was a locking Clinging to your throat Everyplace you move around I'd swin

closer to you Closer get to get closer closer to you If I was a pair of boots I wou

d just bring round your leg When I was dreaming It takes a goody trip I pre

into your lips Closer closer closer to you Closer get to get closer closer to you If I

n your face When you feel the time was right I'd move when you wanted With I

t your bed Right next to your face Begin to make contact Closer closer closer to y

If I had my wishes If I had my way I'd be all the time to you Each and everyu

ish I was a stocking Clinging to your thighs Everytime you move around I'd r

er closer to you Closer got to get closer closer to you If I was a pair of boots I'

ted Just hang round your leg When I am dreaming Wishes many trips If

ssume your lips Closer closer closer to you Closer got to get closer closer to you If

ove your front When you feel the time was right I'd never what you want Wish I

nd your bed Right next to your skin Trying to make contact Closer closer closer to

If I had my wishes If I had my way I'd be all the time to you Each and everyu